New Testament
Interpretation
through
Rhetorical Criticism

GEORGE A. KENNEDY

New Testament Interpretation through Rhetorical Criticism

THE UNIVERSITY OF

NORTH CAROLINA PRESS

CHAPEL HILL AND LONDON

Manufactured in the United States of America

Library of Congress Cataloging in Publication Data

Kennedy, George Alexander, 1928–
New Testament interpretation through rhetorical criticism.

(Studies in religion)
Bibliography: p.
Includes index.
1. Bible. N.T.—Language, style. I. Title.
II. Series: Studies in religion (Chapel Hill, N.C.)
BS2385.K39 1984   225.6'6   83-23577
ISBN 0-8078-1601-9
ISBN 0-8078-4120-X (pbk.)

An earlier version of Chapter Five,
"The Rhetoric of the Gospels," appeared in
Rhetorica I, 2 (1983),
published by the University of California Press.

TO MATTHEW HODGSON

*in appreciation of his friendship
and his contribution to scholarship
during the fifteen years of our
professional association*

Contents

Preface

Although I recognized many years ago that a comprehensive historical understanding of rhetoric must take account of the rhetorical traditions of Christianity, I probably would not have written this book had it not been for a succession of students of biblical literature who have come to me to study rhetoric as a method of interpretation. Yehoshua Gitay was the first, followed by Anthony Lynch, John Levison, and Richard Vinson, and more recently Clifton Black, Jeffrey Gillette, Rollin Grams, Robert Hall, Clarice Martin, and Duane Watson. I have learned much from them, and it was their interest which encouraged me to try to set forth my ideas on the subject in hopes that these would be useful to others. The discussion of Galatians in Chapter 7 is especially indebted to suggestions of Mr. Hall, who read and discussed Betz's commentary with me.

This is not the first time that I have ventured out of my special field of scholarship, and I am very much aware of the dangers involved and of the probability of displaying my ignorance or naïveté on some matters, religious, critical, or historical. To date, biblical scholars have shown a patience notably greater than that of the professional students of some other fields into which I have stumbled. An anonymous reader for The University of North Carolina Press made a number of valuable suggestions and criticisms, and I am greatly indebted as well to Professor Roland M. Frye of the Department of English of the University of Pennsylvania, who read an earlier version of the text and shared generously of his deep understanding of Christianity and criticism. Mrs. Juanita Mason of the staff of the UNC Department of Classics typed and re-typed the manuscript for me efficiently and patiently. Finally, it has been a pleasure to have once again the fine services of

Laura S. Oaks as my editor for The University of North Carolina Press. Her contributions to the book have transcended matters of spelling, punctuation, and format and have in several passages led to the clarification of its ideas.

When modern works are referred to in the text a page reference is given if needed, and full information can be found in the Bibliography.

Chapel Hill, North Carolina
October 1983

New Testament
Interpretation
through
Rhetorical Criticism

In the sermon which I have just completed,
wherever I said Aristotle, I meant Saint Paul.

Attributed to
the Reverend William A. Spooner (1844–1930),
of New College, Oxford

Chapter One. Rhetorical Criticism

The objective of this book is to provide readers of the New Testament with an additional tool of interpretation to complement form criticism, redaction criticism, historical and literary criticism, and other approaches being practiced in the twentieth century. To many biblical scholars rhetoric probably means style, and they may envision in these pages discussion of figures of speech and metaphors not unlike that already to be found in many literary studies of the Scriptures. The identification of rhetoric with style—a feature of what I have elsewhere called *letteraturizza-zione*—is a common phenomenon in the history of the study of rhetoric, but represents a limitation and to some extent a distortion of the discipline of rhetoric as understood and taught in antiquity and by some of the most creative theorists of subsequent periods. Rhetoric is that quality in discourse by which a speaker or writer seeks to accomplish his purposes. Choice and arrangement of words are one of the techniques employed, but what is known in rhetorical theory as "invention"—the treatment of the subject matter, the use of evidence, the argumentation, and the control of emotion—is often of greater importance and is central to rhetorical theory as understood by Greeks and Romans. The writers of the books of the New Testament had a message to convey and sought to persuade an audience to believe it or to believe it more profoundly. As such they are rhetorical, and their methods can be studied by the discipline of rhetoric.

Rhetorical criticism can help to fill a void which lies between form criticism on the one hand and literary criticism on the other. In his 1969 presidential address to the Society of Biblical Literature (since published: see Bibliography), James

Muilenburg called for scholars of the Bible to go beyond form criticism, with its stress upon the typical and the representative, and not to lose sight of "the individual, personal, and unique feature of the particular pericope," in other words to look at passages of Scripture in the persuasive context in which we find them. "It is," he said (p. 5), "the creative synthesis of the particular formulation of the pericope with the content that makes it the distinctive composition it is." Muilenburg rightly labeled such an effort "rhetorical criticism," and he and his students sought to practice it in the study of the Old Testament. In recent years efforts to apply rhetorical criticism to the New Testament have begun to appear (for example in Hans Dieter Betz's commentary on Galatians), but no rigorous methodology has emerged. The outlines of one will be suggested below and its practice illustrated.

How rhetorical criticism differs from form and redaction criticism is perhaps obvious. Form criticism shares with rhetorical criticism an interest in *topoi* or *loci*, but primarily seeks to discover the sources out of which the text is constructed and at its worst seems blind to the finished product. Redaction criticism might be viewed as a special form of rhetorical criticism which deals with texts where the hand of a redactor, or editor, can be detected. It is concerned with the intent of that editor, and especially his theological intent, as revealed in his use of sources. A better understanding of rhetoric and a more systematic rhetorical method may be useful in this process. Rhetorical criticism takes the text as we have it, whether the work of a single author or the product of editing, and looks at it from the point of view of the author's or editor's intent, the unified results, and how it would be perceived by an audience of near contemporaries.

Is this not also what literary criticism does? In my judgment, no. A particularly fine example of recent literary criticism is Northrop Frye's *The Great Code: The Bible and Literature*. Frye freely admits the rhetorical qualities of the Bible: he says that its essential idiom is oratorical; he defines *kerygma* as a mode of rhetoric; he notes the legal metaphor running throughout the Bible; and he gives the subtitle "Rhetoric" to the culminating chapter of his work, suggesting that literary criticism ultimately may lead us to an understanding of rhetoric. But Frye's stance throughout is that of a twentieth-century literary critic. He views the Bible in terms of language and myth as understood in our times; he has less interest in the intent of the biblical writers, more interest in how the Bible was read by great literary geniuses of other times, Dante, Milton, and Blake among them. All of this is immensely interesting, but it is distinct from my goal, which is the more historical one of reading the Bible as it would be read by an early Christian, by an inhabitant of the Greek-speaking world in which rhetoric was the core subject of formal education and in which even those without formal education necessarily developed cultural preconceptions about appropriate discourse.

Rhetoric originates in speech and its primary product is a speech act, not a text, but the rhetoric of historical periods can only be studied through texts. Does this not tend to obscure the difference between rhetorical and literary analysis? To some extent it does, for the rhetorical critic can then do what the literary critic does, turn the pages back and forth to compare earlier passages with later ones and subject the text to the kind of detailed analysis which a hearer of a speech cannot possibly undertake. A speech is linear and cumulative, and any context in it can only be perceived in contrast to what has gone before, especially what has immediately gone before, though a very able speaker lays the ground for what he intends to say later and has a total unity in mind when he first begins to speak. We need to keep in mind that the Bible in early Christian times was more often heard when read aloud to a group than read privately; very few early Christians owned copies of the Bible, and some did not know how to read. To a greater extent than any modern text, the Bible retained an oral and linear quality for its audience. True, it was read again and again and thus took on the qualities of a frozen oral text in which a hearer might remember passages yet to come, and sometimes it was read in pericopes rather than continuously through a book.

Some of the writers of books of the New Testament show signs of envisioning this, but the rhetorical qualities inherent in the text were originally intended to have an impact on first hearing and to be heard by a group. In practicing rhetorical criticism we need to keep in mind that intent and that original impact, and thus to read the Bible as speech.

The primary field of rhetoric in Greece and Rome was in civic life, and it is legal and political rhetoric that is largely described in classical handbooks of the subject. Most modern critics, however, recognize that there is a distinctive rhetoric of religion. It can be found in many cultures, East and West, and at the heart of it lies authoritative proclamation, not rational persuasion. Those who accept religious teachings generally do so because of their perception of certain qualities in the person who utters them and because of their intuitive response to the message. Absolute demands, deliberate rejection of worldly reason, sometimes paradoxes or even obscurity, become a persuasive factor in the enunciation of a new religious message. This phenomenon is often known as "sacred language." In a recent important work on the philosophy of rhetoric, Ernesto Grassi (pp. 103–4) summarizes the rhetoric of sacred language as embodying five characteristics. (1) It has a purely revealing or evangelical character, not a demonstrative or proving function; it does not arise out of a process of inference, but authoritatively proclaims the truth. (2) Its statements are immediate, formulated without mediation or contemplation. (3) They are imagistic and metaphorical, lending the reality of sensory appearances a new meaning. (4) Its assertions are absolute and urgent; whatever does not fit with them is treated as outrageous. (5) Its pronouncements are outside of time. Rational speech, such as the civic rhetoric of Greek cities, is in contrast demonstrative, based on formally valid inference from accepted premises.

This distinctive religious rhetoric can, of course, be found in the Bible. Jesus' message was essentially proclaimed, not argued on the basis of probability, and that is why it is often called by the Greek word for proclamation, *kerygma*. But neither the Old nor the New Testament is pure sacred language in the way that the utterances of an Indian guru or a Greek oracle are. Very often, even in old parts of the Bible, something is added which seems to give a reason why the proclamation should be received and thus appeals, at least in part, to human rationality. The Ten Commandments (Exod. 20:2–17) furnish an excellent example. The first five commandments are all accompanied by some kind of reason why the commandment should be accepted. The reason may be historical evidence, acceptable on the basis of the experience of the audience, as in the first commandment: "I am the Lord your God"; the evidence, "who brought you out of the land of Egypt, out of the house of bondage"; therefore, "You shall have no other gods before me." In the second commandment, the reason is a threat, "You shall not make for yourself a graven image . . . ; for I the Lord your God am a jealous God visiting the iniquity of the fathers upon the children of the third and fourth generation," followed by a promise to love those who will keep the commandment. In classical rhetoric such a statement with a supporting reason is called an *enthymeme*. The elaboration of the thought in the second and fourth commandments is a form of "amplification" and has a rhetorical function, for dwelling on the thought helps to prove it or to seem to prove it. The last five commandments are not enthymemes, but the reasons given in the first five have established an authoritative pattern so that further evidence is less necessary. We shall see that there is much use of enthymemes in the New Testament as well, though sacred language also is to be found. When a doctrine is purely proclaimed and not couched in enthymemes I call the technique *radical Christian rhetoric*. This is characteristic not only of some individual pericopes, but of entire books such as the Gospel of Mark.

Another feature of radical Christian rhetoric which is an inheritance of the Old Testament is the doctrine that the speaker is a vehicle of God's will. Something like it is also found in Greece, where early poets claimed that the gods spoke through them without conscious effort on their part (as

in Hesiod *Theogony* 21–35; Plato *Ion* 534d). The communications between God, Moses, Pharaoh, and the people in the
first half of the book of Exodus will repay careful study by
every student of the rhetoric of the Bible. Moses here does not
persuade Pharaoh in the way a classical orator would appeal to
him. He does not argue that to let his people go is in accordance with common principles of justice and in the long-term
best interests of Pharaoh himself. He speaks words God has
given him and performs miracles, while God alternately hard-
ens and softens Pharaoh's heart. The ultimate escape of the
people is the result of God's action, not of Moses', or Aaron's,
persuasive abilities. Christianity applied this idea to its teaching of the Holy Spirit and of the Grace of God. "It is not you
who will speak," Jesus says to his disciples, "but the Holy
Spirit" (Mark 13:11; see also Matthew 10:19–20). The Christian
orator, like his Jewish predecessor, is a vehicle of God's will to
whom God will supply the necessary words, and his audience
will be persuaded, or not persuaded, not because of the capaci-
ties of their minds to understand the message, but because of
God's love for them which allows their hearts to be moved or
withholds that grace. Paul writes to the Corinthians (1 Cor.
2:13) that "we impart this in words not taught by human wisdom but taught by the Spirit, interpreting spiritual truths to
those who possess the Spirit."

Rhetoric is a historical phenomenon and differs somewhat
from culture to culture, more in matters of arrangement and
style than in basic devices of invention. The New Testament
lies on the cusp between Jewish and Greek culture; the life and
religious traditions it depicts are Jewish, its language is Greek.
How legitimate is it to approach the New Testament in terms
of Greek ideas of rhetoric?

By the time of Christ the culture of the Near East had been
undergoing a gradual process of Hellenization for three hun-
dred years. Jewish thought absorbed some features of Greek
culture, of which the works of Josephus and Philo give striking
evidence, and the books of the New Testament were written in
Greek to be read by or to speakers of Greek, many of them

with some experience of Greek education. Rhetoric was a systematic academic discipline universally taught throughout the Roman empire. It represented approximately the level of high-school education today and was, indeed, the exclusive subject of secondary education. Before taking up rhetoric a student had often spent several years studying grammar. Palestine and Syria were not rhetorical backwaters: one of the most famous rhetoricians of the first century before Christ, Theodorus, was a native of Gadara who moved to Rome, where he became the teacher of the emperor Tiberius, and then settled in Rhodes. Jews sometimes studied rhetoric. The most famous rhetorician of the reign of Augustus was a Sicilian Jew named Caecilius of Calacte. The greatest rhetorician of the second century of the Christian era was Hermogenes, who was born in Tarsus, the home of Saint Paul, and who taught in the cities of the Ionian coast, where Christian churches had an early development.

After completing their study of rhetoric some students went on to study philosophy, in which dialectic was regarded as the initial stage. Dialectic and rhetoric overlap in their use of logical argument, but differ in form; a dialectical dispute is cast as a question-and-answer dialogue, whereas rhetoric utilizes continuous discourse. In his debates with the Pharisees (for example, Matt. 22) Jesus shows considerable dialectical skill, whether intuitively apprehended or learned by observation of disputation among the rabbis. Luke (2:46) apparently thought Jesus learned something about dialectic on a visit to Jerusalem at the age of twelve. Paul encountered debates in Corinth (1 Cor. 1:20) and doubtless elsewhere.

It is not a necessary premise of this study that the evangelists or Saint Paul had formally studied Greek rhetoric. In the case of Paul the evidence is somewhat ambivalent. Shown in Acts 22 speaking Hebrew in Jerusalem, he is made to stress his education in Jerusalem according to strict Jewish law, which might seem to rule out formal study of Greek inasmuch as that involved intensive reading in pagan authors, and in 2 Corinthians 11:6 he humbly grants what others had apparently said, that he is unskilled in speaking. But he is certainly thoroughly at home in the Greek idiom of his time and in the conventions of the Greek epistle, and when addressing Greeks he is able to make reference to classical literature (Acts 17:28; 1 Cor. 15:33; Titus 1:12). Even if he had not studied in a Greek school, there were many handbooks of rhetoric in common circulation which he could have seen. He and the evangelists as well would, indeed, have been hard put to escape an awareness of rhetoric as practiced in the culture around them, for the rhetorical theory of the schools found its immediate application in almost every form of oral and written communication: in official documents and public letters, in private correspondence, in the lawcourts and assemblies, in speeches at festivals and commemorations, and in literary composition in both prose and verse. In addressing a Greek audience, even when he pointedly rejected the "wisdom of this world," Paul could not expect to be persuasive unless there was some overlap between the content and form of what he said and the expectations of his audience. What we need to do is to try to hear his words as a Greek-speaking audience would have heard them, and that involves some understanding of classical rhetoric.

Approaching the New Testament through classical rhetoric is thus historically justified. It is also philosophically justifiable. Though rhetoric is colored by the traditions and conventions of the society in which it is applied, it is also a universal phenomenon which is conditioned by basic workings of the human mind and heart and by the nature of all human society. Aristotle's objective in writing his *Rhetoric* was not to describe Greek rhetoric, but to describe this universal facet of human communication. The categories he identifies are intended to exhaust the possibilities, though the examples of them which he gives are drawn from the specific practice of a Greek city state. It is perfectly possible to utilize the categories of Aristotelian rhetoric to study speech in China, India, Africa, and elsewhere in the world, cultures much more different from the Greek than was that of Palestine in the time of the Roman empire. What is unique about Greek rhetoric, and what makes it useful for criticism, is the degree to which it was conceptualized. The Greeks gave names to rhetorical techniques, many of which are found all over the world. They organized these techniques into a system which could be taught and learned. What we mean by classical rhetorical theory is this structured system which describes the universal phenomenon of rhetoric in Greek terms. Before rhetoric was conceptualized the Greeks practiced it and learned it by imitation with little conscious effort. Though the Jews of the pre-Christian era seem never to have conceptualized rhetoric to any significant degree, the importance of speech among them is everywhere evident in the Old Testament, and undoubtedly they learned its techniques by imitation. In understanding how their rhetoric worked we have little choice but to employ the concepts and terms of the Greeks.

The Fathers of the Church were in much the same position as we in trying to talk about the rhetoric of the Bible; they were forced to use Greek terms to describe the various techniques and literary forms found therein. The fullest example of this is Saint Augustine's splendid work *On Christian Doctrine*, which provides the preacher with necessary skills of hermeneutics and homiletics, and which in its fourth book analyzes the eloquence of passages of Scripture, showing that they attain or surpass classical standards. Augustine, and several others of the Fathers of the Church, had not only studied classical rhetoric but taught it before their conversion.

In his important work *Chiasmus in the New Testament*, Nils Wilhelm Lund lamented (p. 8) the practice of applying the terminology of classical rhetoric to the Bible: "Whenever the purely classical standards are employed in appraising the New Testament, its style is found wanting. Modern classicists agree in this respect with the conclusion of the early Fathers of the Church." And again (p. 23), "The procedure was misleading, since it set up Greek rhetoric as the only standard by which these writings were to be judged. . . . Whatever does not fall into its categories is either described as the natural eloquence of the heart or is dismissed as crude and unfinished." Specifically, Lund was trying to explain the neglect of understanding of *chiasmus* (the reversal of the order in corresponding words or phrases) on the part of Biblical scholars, but there is some broader truth in his observation. The problem is not so much the utilization of classical rhetoric as the rather limited view of classical rhetoric taken by the Fathers and by modern critics, an identification of rhetoric with style and especially with Attic diction and with the ornamentation provided by figures of speech. If rhetorical criticism is to be valid, it must be practiced with some awareness of the traditions of Jewish speech, of which chiasmus is one, and if it is to be useful it must embrace more than style. If fundamental and universal features of rhetoric are kept in mind and if we seek to use them in describing the logical and structural features of the text before us, rather than simply quarrying a text for examples of classical figures, we can significantly enhance our appreciation of its meaning without violence to the author's intent. The ultimate goal of rhetorical analysis, briefly put, is the discovery of the author's intent and of how that is transmitted through a text to an audience.

The basic theoretical concepts underlying classical rhetoric are enunciated by Aristotle in his *Rhetoric*, which represents his lectures in Athens in the mid–fourth century and is partly based on principles laid down by Plato in the *Phaedrus*. During the next several centuries a large number of treatises and handbooks on rhetoric were written in Greek and Latin, intended for the use of teachers and students. The most important of the few which have survived are the *Rhetoric to Herennius*, in Latin but directly based on Greek sources and probably written by an otherwise unknown Cornificius about 84 B.C., Cicero's early work *On Invention* and his *Partitions of Oratory*, and the large treatise of Quintilian, *On the Education of the Orator*, written in Rome between A.D. 92 and 95. These works will be the most convenient sources of technical information for most students of rhetoric in the New Testament, and all are available in English translation with notes and indices (see Bibliography). Quintilian regularly summarizes the theories of earlier writers, including many whose works are now lost, as understood in the period of composition of the New Testament. Cicero's other writings on rhetoric—*On the Orator*, *Brutus*, *The Orator*, and *Topics*—are helpful in gaining insight into how rhetoric was perceived in the first century before Christ. The serious student of the subject should also be aware of the existence of two modern compilations of the theory in German, *Handbuch der literarischen Rhetorik* by Heinrich Lausberg, and *Antike Rhetorik: Technik und Methode* by Josef Martin, and much valuable information, together with critical application to texts in English, can be found in Edward P. J. Corbett's *Classical Rhetoric for the Modern Student*. My own books that trace the historical development of classical rhetorical theory and practice are identified in the Bibliography.

Rhetoric is defined by Aristotle (1.2.1355b) as the faculty of discovering in each case the available means of persuasion, and by Quintilian (2.15.38) as *scientia bene dicendi*, the knowledge of how to speak well. The two definitions represent a difference in emphasis, by Aristotle on proof, by Quintilian on a variety of rhetorical features which does not neglect proof, but gives increased attention to style.

Rhetoric as taught in the schools consisted of five parts which recapitulate five stages in the act of composing a speech. Most rhetorical handbooks are primarily intended to train a student to speak in a court of law, but it is not difficult to use them as a basis of analysis of other forms of discourse; this was in fact done by ancient critics like Demetrius, Dionysius of Halicarnassus, and Longinus, who even illustrates his theory of sublimity by citing the first chapter of Genesis (*On Sublimity* 9.9). The five parts of rhetoric are *invention*, which deals with the planning of a discourse and the arguments to be used in it; *arrangement*, the composition of the various parts into an effective whole; *style*, which involves both choice of words and the composition of words into sentences, including the use of figures; *memory*, or preparation for delivery; and *delivery*, the rules for control of the voice and the use of gestures. These are universal categories, not peculiar to Greek rhetoric. Discussion of memory and delivery is often omitted in the handbooks and will be omitted here, for they relate to oral presentation, about which we know little. It may be helpful, however, to summarize briefly what was taught in New Testament times on the subjects of invention, arrangement, and style, applied both to oral speech and to written composition.

Invention is based either on external proofs, which the author uses but does not invent, the evidence of witnesses, for example, or of documents; or on internal or "artistic" proof, which the author is said to invent. In the New Testament there are three common forms of external proof: quotations of Scripture, the evidence of miracles, and the naming of witnesses, such as John the Baptist or the disciples of Jesus. The evangelists and Saint Paul frequently cite prophecies of the Old Testament which are fulfilled in the coming of Jesus, and they occasionally cite the Old Testament as evidence on other matters, for example the law. Even Satan quotes Scripture to make a point (Matt. 4:6). Such evidence is "external" in the sense that it is not a creation of the mind of the speaker, though he has chosen and utilized it and may sometimes build a logical argument upon it. Evidence from Scripture, which Christian preachers have continued to use throughout the centuries, has the advantage of being familiar to the audience and authoritative. Because it is external it seems to be objective, though in fact much subjectivity is involved in the choice of passages cited. Jesus' fulfillment of Old Testament prophecy is primarily used to endow him with authority, which in turn makes it possible for him to make new commandments.

The miracles performed by Jesus, and to some extent by the apostles as well, function in a similar way as external evidence. Before giving the Sermon on the Mount, Jesus is described as moving through a crowd healing the sick. This action, which is external to his sermon and to which he does not refer in it, should be viewed as greatly increasing his authority when he does speak. After the sermon he performs another miracle, thus confirming his power. The ordinary New Testament term for a miracle is *semeion*, or sign, and signs are mentioned by Paul as the characteristic form of evidence among the Jews in contrast to wisdom (logical proof) among the Greeks: "For Jews demand signs and Greeks seek wisdom, but we preach Christ crucified" (1 Cor. 1:22–23). *Semeion* is a term of Aristotelian rhetoric as well (1.2.1357b), but is used there to mean a probable or necessary cause for an inference: if a man is just, it is a *sign* that he is wise; if it is raining, it is a *sign* there are clouds.

There are three universal factors in any rhetorical or persuasive situation: a speaker or writer, an audience, and a discourse. (Rhetoricians since the eighteenth century have added a fourth, the occasion or context in which the work is composed or delivered.) According to Aristotle (1.2.1356a) there are also three and only three modes of artistic proof: *ethos, pathos,* and *logos.* These categories are found in the speech of all cultures and they inhere respectively in speaker, audience, and discourse. Ethos means "character" and may be defined as the credibility that the author or speaker is able to establish in his work. The audience is induced to trust what he says because they trust him, as a good man or an expert on the subject. In Aristotelian theory ethos is something entirely internal to a speech, but in practice the authority which the speaker brings to the occasion is an important factor, and this is especially true in the New Testament. Pathos inheres in the audience and may be defined as the emotional reactions the hearers undergo as the orator "plays upon their feelings." In the New Testament its commonest form is the promise of eternal life or threat of damnation, though it appears in subtler forms as well, as in the Beatitudes. Logos refers to the logical argument found within the discourse. In classical rhetoric logos is ordinarily regarded as probable argument, not logical certainty, but Christians came to regard the arguments of Scripture as divinely revealed and thus certain.

Logical argument is of two forms, either inductive, which uses a series of examples to point to a general conclusion, or deductive, which enunciates premises probably acceptable to an audience and draws a deductive conclusion from the premises. The examples (*paradeigmata*) used in inductive argument are drawn from myth or from nature or other sources. In the New Testament they are most commonly taken from Jewish history or from everyday life and nature. The parables of Jesus are inductive in method, sometimes listing several examples from which a conclusion can be drawn, but rarely making the conclusion explicit before a general audience. Deductive proof in rhetoric is called the *enthymeme*. An enthymeme commonly takes the form of a statement and a supporting reason, as in "Blessed are the poor in spirit, for theirs is the kingdom of heaven" (Matt. 5:3). The word "for" in English, *gar* or *hoti* in Greek, is commonly the indication of an enthymeme. Behind any enthymeme stands a logical syllogism. "Those who receive the kingdom of heaven are blessed" would be the major premise, universal and positive, acceptable by definition. "The poor in spirit will receive the kingdom of heaven" would then be the minor premise. This would not be an acceptable premise to a sophisticated classical audience, but it probably was acceptable to Jesus' audience. It is an example of a premise couched in sacred language. Even if, at this point in his speech, the audience did not believe it was true, many of them would have liked to believe that it was true. Its probability is strengthened by the overall consistency of Jesus' message, in which each enunciation is supported by every other enunciation, but is also greatly facilitated by the growing authority of Jesus, in the final result by his being the Messiah and the Son of God. If the premises are then accepted, the conclusion follows by exclusion of the middle term, "the kingdom of heaven": thus, the poor in spirit are blessed. More will be said in Chapter 2 about the rhetorical qualities of this enthymeme.

Except in tightly reasoned philosophical argument to a peer group, speakers and writers do not generally employ a full statement of major premise, minor premise, and conclusion, which would constitute what is known in logic as a syllogism or in rhetoric as an *epicheireme*. They assume, suppress, or imply one of the parts, as Jesus does, and thus they speak enthymematically. Enthymemes take one of two forms. They may be categorical, based on a definition as is the one just cited, or hypothetical: "If your right eye causes you to sin, pluck it out and throw it away; [for] it is better that you lose one of your members than that your whole body be thrown into Hell" (Matt. 5:29). Either form may be conjunctive or disjunctive: "No one can serve two masters; for either he will hate the one and love the other, or he will be devoted to the one and despise the other" (Matt. 6:24). An enthymeme is often supported by a maxim (*gnome* or *sententia*), as Jesus does in the passage just cited: "You cannot serve God and Mammon."

It was obviously Aristotle's intention to encourage the use of logically valid proof in oratory. Greek oratory is certainly far more logical than the arguments to be found in the Bible, but even Greek oratory, especially in contexts other than a lawcourt, contains strong subjective elements. An audience is regularly asked to make a judgment or take an action on the basis of values which they hold. For example, in his great speech *On the Crown*, Demosthenes, being in a rather weak legal position, devotes much of his time to showing that the actions he has taken were consistent with Athenian values that left him little choice. It is very commonly the case that logical arguments are introduced into a speech only to support details or to give an appearance of reason or to justify a decision which is in fact made largely on the basis of ethos or pathos. The same is almost always the case in religious discourse, because the premises of argument are usually based on a scriptural authority or personal intuition, enunciated in sacred language. Matthew and Paul make extensive use of the *forms* of logical argument, but the *validity* of their arguments is entirely dependent on their assumptions, which cannot be logically and objectively proved. To a nonbeliever they may seem totally invalid, but much the same might be said of the arguments of a democratic political speaker in the eyes of a person who does not believe in democracy. The validity of both democracy and Christianity is personal and experiential.

Aristotle's theory of three modes of proof—logical, ethical, and pathetical—was converted by Cicero (*Orator* 69) into three *officia oratoris*, or duties of the orator: to teach, to please, and to move. Cicero thus recognized that logical argument is rarely enough to persuade an audience. He is followed in this by Quintilian (12.10.58–59) and Saint Augustine (*On Christian Doctrine* 4.27–29). Augustine explains that the Christian orator needs to please in order to maintain the interest of his audience, that they may be moved to action. Speaking to please is of course a somewhat slippery game, often associated with sophists. Plato and Aristotle both warn against it, and Saint Paul specifically rejects it (as in 1 Thess. 2:4). In its more objectionable form it determines the content of what is said; this seems totally lacking in the New Testament. Its more acceptable form is the use of a style pleasing to the audience, for example in Luke's account of the Nativity or in Paul's encomium of charity in 1 Corinthians 13.

Inventional theory after Aristotle, but before the first century of the Christian era, was much complicated by the development of what is known as stasis theory. A speaker in planning a speech, or a critic in analyzing it, was encouraged to define the *stasis*, or basic issue of the case. There are four main forms of stasis: fact (also known as conjecture), definition, quality, and jurisdiction; but there is also a parallel set of categories known as legal questions. The simplest version of the matter is probably that in Quintilian 3.6, but a more systematic account is that of Hermogenes in his treatise *On Stases* (see Bibliography). The issue is one of fact if the central question is whether something was done at all, or was done by a specific person at a specific time: "Did Jesus heal on the Sabbath?" involves stasis of fact. The question is one of definition if the facts are admitted, but there is disagreement about the definition of the terms: "What constitutes healing?" or "Who is my neighbor?" (Luke 10:29–37). The question is one of quality if facts and definitions are admitted by all parties, but the action is justified on other grounds: "Is it right to break the law in order to heal on the Sabbath?" In stasis of jurisdiction a speaker rejects the right of a tribunal to make a judgment, which is perhaps implied in Stephen's speech to the Council in Acts 7. In a legal question there is an expressed doubt about a law itself, for example about the difference between its wording and intent. The law might prohibit a variety of activities on the Sabbath but not specifically mention healing: "Was it the intent of the law to prevent healing?" Stasis can often be found in Jesus' debates with the Pharisees, in speeches in Acts, and in Paul's epistles.

There are three *species* of rhetoric, a theory formulated by Aristotle (3.1.1358a) and universally found in subsequent writers: *judicial*, *deliberative*, and *epideictic*. Although these categories specifically refer to the circumstances of classical civic oratory, they are in fact applicable to all discourse. The species is judicial when the author is seeking to persuade the audience to make a judgment about events occurring in the past; it is deliberative when he seeks to persuade them to take some action in the future; it is epideictic when he seeks to persuade them to hold or reaffirm some point of view in the present, as when he celebrates or denounces some person or some quality. Praise or blame is taken by Aristotle to be the characteristic feature of epideictic. In a single discourse there is sometimes utilization of more than one species, and the definition of the species as a whole can become very difficult, but a discourse usually has one dominant species which reflects the author's major purpose in speaking or writing. The Sermon on the Mount as well as some other discourses of Jesus and some epistles are predominantly deliberative; some speeches in Acts and 2 Corinthians are judicial; the Magnificat (Luke 1:46–55) and Jesus' consolation of his disciples in John 14–17 are predominantly epideictic. Determination of the species sometimes helps to bring out the emphases of a work and thus the intent of the author. In judicial the basic argument involves the question of truth or justice; in deliberative, the question of self-interest and future benefits; in epideictic, a change of attitude or deepening of values such as the honorable and the good, or in a Christian context, belief and faith. The three species have both positive and negative forms: prosecution and defense (or apology); exhortation and dissuasion; encomium and invective.

In constructing arguments, both inductive and deductive, a speaker makes use of "topics," *topoi* or *loci*. They are the "places" where he looks for something to say about his subject. In the *Rhetoric* Aristotle discusses topics from three points of view. "Common" topics (in sixteenth- to eighteenth-century English, "commonplaces") can be used in any species of discourse, and four groups are distinguished: the possible and impossible, past fact, future fact, and degree (*Rhetoric* 2.19). These can all be found in the New Testament. The impossible: "No man can serve two masters" (Matt. 6:24). Past fact: "By faith Abel offered to God a more acceptable sacrifice than Cain" (Heb. 11:4). Future fact: "Many will come in my name, saying, 'I am he!' and they will lead many astray" (Mark 13:6). Past fact leading to the topic of degree: "While we were yet sinners Christ died for us. Since, therefore, we are now justified by his blood, much more shall we be saved by him from the wrath of God" (Rom. 5:8–9). This type of *a fortiori* argument is commonly known as "the more and the less."

A second kind of topic (*Rhetoric* 1.4–8) might be called "material" and is specific to the species of oratory. For example, a deliberative speaker in a political context deals with the topics of ways and means, war and peace, defense, imports and exports, and legislation. These furnish materials out of which he can construct his headings. In the context of the New Testament, the writer's material topics become his propositions; these he then amplifies or works out in the body of his work. A good example are the definitions given in the opening verses of John's Gospel, which are then developed through the work. "Messiah" is a topic in this sense; so are "Son of God," "faith," "hope," and "love."

The third kind of topic is "strategical" and, as discussed by Aristotle (*Rhetoric* 2.23), bears some similarity to the topic of degree. Such topics are common to all species of discourse and provide strategies of argument. For example, since by the law of contradictories opposites cannot both be true, a speaker can establish a proposition by rephrasing it in the negative and producing an example to refute the negative. Jesus does this repeatedly: "In my Father's house are many rooms; if it were not so, I would have told you" (John 14:2).

Aristotle's lengthy treatise *Topics* organizes the strategical topics more systematically. He finds the logical basis of topics in his theory of logical categories (1.9.103b): substance, quantity, quality, relation, place, time, condition, state, activity, and passivity. These provide predicates for four sources of argument (1.13.105a): (1) *The provision of propositions by means of definition, genus, property, and accident*. For example, "I am the light of the world; he who follows me will not walk in darkness, but will have the light of life" (John 8:12) utilizes definition and property. (2) *The distinction of how many different ways a thing can be said*. This is less common in the New Testament, but can be seen in reinterpretation of words of the law: "For he is not a real Jew who is one outwardly, nor is true circumcision something external and physical" (Rom. 2:28). (3) *The discovery of differences*. In the parable of the sower, the seed falls on different kinds of ground which produce different results. (4) *Utilization of similarity*. This is a common topic of Jesus' parables: "With what can we compare the kingdom of God, or what parable shall we use for it? It is like a grain of mustard seed . . . ," with amplification of the comparison (Mark 4:30–31). Understanding of the theory of topics after Aristotle is best seen in Cicero's *Topics* and in the influential treatise of Boethius, *De Topicis Differentiis*.

Most of what goes on in rhetorical composition is *amplification* of the basic thesis of the speaker by means of the topics which he has chosen to utilize in support of it. This process is necessitated by the oral nature of the situation and by the constraints on the audience. A philosopher or scientist might be able to state a thesis and the evidence for it and expect a learned reader to be persuaded, but even a learned audience has difficulty taking in such a proof on one hearing, and a general audience will not understand even a simpler thesis when barely sketched. The speaker must therefore develop his subject repeating his basic ideas several times in different words, illustrating what he means, relating it in some way to the experience of his audience. All speech thus involves the "working out" (*ergasia*) of its inventional topics. Techniques of logical argument like the enthymeme and example are useful in this process, but so are devices of style, especially figures of thought, which awaken audience interest and allow them to see the material in new ways, and ethos and pathos play a role as well. Ethos should not generally be confined to a single self-revelation at the beginning of the speech, but should be maintained throughout both by what the speaker says and how he says it, and pathos can be built up by the emotional ideas and words used in the course of the speech and not reserved for a final appeal. An excellent example of *ergasia* is found in the opening chapters of 1 Corinthians, where Paul develops his authoritative ethos and lays a theological basis for his subsequent admonitions to the Corinthians by working out and reiterating a small number of concepts which are the "topics" of his invention.

In the later stages of their training under a grammarian and in the early stages of rhetorical study, students in New Testament times and late antiquity practiced exercises in composition called *progymnasmata*, which provided a method for working out the common types of discourse. If students subsequently undertook serious literary work, they tended to utilize progymnasmatic forms in the development of their thought. Because these forms are common types, found in many cultures, something analogous to them can often be found in the Bible, though they are rarely developed there in accord with the specific suggestions of the Greek and Roman schools. The parables of Jesus correspond to what was taught in the schools as *mythos*, for which the fables of Aesop were the standard classical models; this was regarded as the simplest and easiest of the exercises. There were also exercises in narrative, in encomium and invective, and in the demonstration and refutation of a thesis. Similar compositional units can often be found in the New Testament. The exercise called *chria* involved telling an anecdote about what someone did or said and then explaining its meaning and amplifying it. Holy Communion in the Christian Church is a ritual elaboration of a chria: while reading the text, the priest reenacts what Jesus did and said at the Last Supper. *Prosopopoeia* was an exercise in writing a speech for some mythological or historical personage, exhibiting his character. The speeches in the first chapter of Luke are probably prosopopoeiae; one of the most difficult questions in rhetorical criticism of the New Testament is whether the discourses of Jesus and the speakers in Acts should also be viewed in this light. *Synkrisis* was an exercise comparing two individuals or things: 2 Corinthians 3:7–18 could be described as a synkrisis of Moses and Paul. *Ecphrasis*, a vivid portrayal of a scene, well describes some of the visions in the Apocalypse. These terms will occasionally be useful in identifying compositional units in the New Testament.

The second part of rhetoric, arrangement, seeks to determine the rhetorically effective composition of the speech and mold its elements into a unified structure. In the *Phaedrus* (264c) Plato says that every discourse should be like a living body in which the parts cohere like limbs. Under arrangement it is convenient to discuss the conventional parts of an oration, though in practice classical rhetoricians usually find it necessary to do that as part of their survey of invention.

Judicial oratory provides the fullest conventional structure, and in an established order, but something like it can often be found in other persuasive speaking and writing. A judicial speech usually begins with a *proem* or *exordium* which seeks to obtain the attention of the audience and goodwill or sympathy toward the speaker. It then proceeds to a *narration* of the facts, or background information, and states the *proposition* which the speaker wishes to prove, often with a *partition* of it into separate headings. The speaker then presents his arguments in the *proof*, followed by a *refutation* of opposing views; here he may incorporate what was called a *digression*, often a relevant examination of motivations or attendant circumstances. Finally comes an *epilogue* or *peroration*, which summarizes the argument and seeks to arouse the emotions of the audience to take action or make judgment.

The deliberative structure is usually a simplified version of the judicial: proem, proposition, proof, and epilogue. Occasionally a narration is employed; when it does occur, it is often after rather than before the proposition. The proof is divided up into a series of headings, treating the various material topics. The term "heading" (*kephalaion*) came into regular use among Greek rhetoricians of the Roman empire. Though not commonly used by modern rhetorical critics, it is a convenient label for this kind of division of the subject. The first heading of the Sermon on the Mount, for example, takes up the topic of murder and develops it into a heading against anger.

In epideictic the body of the speech between proem and epilogue is usually devoted to an orderly sequence of amplified topics dealing with the life of the person being celebrated or with the qualities of the concept under consideration, often adorned with vivid description (ecphrasis) or with a comparison of the subject to something else (synkrisis). More will be said about the form of epideictic in Chapter 3.

The first chapter of 1 Corinthians provides a convenient example of rhetorical arrangement and of how the concept can be applied to the composition of something other than a speech. After a formal salutation, which is amplified with topics important for the ethos and logos of the letter, Paul begins with a proem (1:4–9) revealing none of his anxiety about the Corinthians and aiming to secure their goodwill. He follows this in verse 10 with the proposition of the entire letter, summarized in a single sentence. Then comes a brief narration

(11–12) explaining the background event which has prompted him to write. This leads immediately into argumentation of a defensive sort which could be regarded as a refutation of the charge that he himself is responsible for problems in Corinth (12–17). Then he turns in verse 18 to begin working out the topics which will be fundamental to his latter argument. The chapter ends with an emotional statement (30) supported by the external evidence of Scripture (31).

The third part of rhetoric is style. In periods of mannerism style can become a matter of gratuitous ornamentation and conceit, but in the best writers and as understood by the best critics, it is functional and varies with the author's intent. It is one of his persuasive tools. Aristotle devotes much of the third book of his *Rhetoric* to style and insists that its fundamental "virtue" should be clarity, though he mentions various other qualities which style may take on. These observations were systematized by his successor Theophrastus into four virtues: correctness, clarity, ornamentation, and propriety. Correctness is a matter of grammar; clarity, of the expression and arrangement of ideas. Ornamentation in a functional sense is the use of devices such as figures of speech to amplify the topics, to give emphasis and distinction to the thought, or to maintain contact with the audience. Propriety is achieved by matching the style to the content, speaking of simple subjects in simple words and of lofty thoughts with dignity.

Many classical critics set forth a theory of three levels of style: the plain, the grand, and the middle, the middle sometimes thought of as aiming at smoothness, whereas the grand style may be abrupt or violent. Cicero in *The Orator* and Saint Augustine in the fourth book of *On Christian Doctrine* closely associate the three styles with the three duties of the orator: to teach in the plain style, to please in the middle style, and to move in the grand style. More complicated classifications of styles can be found in the treatise of Demetrius *On Style* (per-

haps third century before Christ), in the critical writings of
Dionysius of Halicarnassus (first century before Christ), and
in the treatise of Hermogenes *On Ideas of Style* (second century
after Christ). Hermogenes' became the fundamental treatment
of the subject for late Greek and Byzantine teachers of rhetoric
and was applied by them to the study of the Bible and the
Fathers of the Church. In this process some Byzantine critics
came to value "obscurity" as a Christian virtue of style and to
see in Christian writing of an obscure sort a quality they called
emphasis, which involved meaning more than one said. The
opening of the Gospel of John might be taken as an example.

The theory of style as a whole is divided into two parts. First
comes *lexis* (diction), which deals with choice of words. The
most precise term in common usage is said to be the "proper"
word in any context, but to create varying effects the author
may prefer archaic or rare words, or make use of foreign
words, or occasionally may coin new words, something not
difficult to do in Greek, where new words can be created by
the compounding of simple words. Early Christians had new
thoughts to express, and their verbal resources were often
taxed. They had to use old words in new ways—"the kingdom
of heaven," for example—sometimes borrowing meanings
from Hebrew traditions, sometimes from Greek usages (as
with the concept of the Logos). The greatest resource for the
forceful expression of original thought is the metaphor, and
much can be learned about a speaker's assumptions and about
his understanding of his audience from his choice and use of
metaphor. The New Testament is rich in metaphor, of which
some of the most striking instances are the first-person assertions of John's Gospel, "I am the true vine, and my Father is
the vinedresser," among many other examples. Metaphor is
one of several devices known collectively as *tropes*, or "turn-
ings," by which one word is substituted for another. Other
tropes include *synecdoche* (part for the whole, or the opposite),
metonymy (a proper instead of a common noun), and *hyperbole*
(an exaggerated metaphor). An unintentional mistake in the
use of a word is called a barbarism, but a deliberate misuse of a

single word becomes the trope *catachresis*, or *abusio*. In the Bible this chiefly occurs when there is no Greek word for a Hebrew term. *Ouranos*, the Greek word for the deified sky, applied to Heaven despite its pagan association, might be taken as an example. Quintilian discusses tropes in 8.6. Examples of most can be found in the New Testament. In his treatise *On Figures and Tropes*, written about A.D. 700, the Venerable Bede draws all his examples from the Bible. Although the terminology of classical theories of diction continues in some use, modern theories of language have gone far deeper into an understanding of the subject. An excellent introduction is supplied by G. B. Caird's *The Language and Imagery of the Bible*.

The second part of style is *synthesis*, the study of composition, the way words are put together to form phrases, clauses, or sentences. The most studied aspect of composition is the use of *figures*, both figures of speech and figures of thought. Figures differ from tropes in that they involve more than one word, and a mistake in composition is known as a solecism rather than a barbarism. Figures of speech result from manipulation of the sound or arrangement of words in the context. A common one is *anaphora*, the use of the same word to begin a series of clauses or sentences, as is done with the word "blessed" in the Beatitudes. Anaphora is like a series of hammer blows in which the repetition of the word both connects and reenforces the successive thoughts. A figure of thought is an unexpected change in syntax or an arrangement of the ideas, as opposed to the words, within a sentence, which calls attention to itself. *Antithesis* is a figure of thought involving arrangement: "You have heard that it was said, 'You shall love your neighbor and hate your enemy.' But I say to you, Love your enemies and pray for those who persecute you" (Matt. 5:43–44); *rhetorical question* one involving syntax: "But if the salt has lost its taste, how shall its saltiness be restored?" (Matt. 5:13). Another common figure of thought is *apostrophe*, in which the speaker suddenly makes a direct appeal to someone, as Jesus does in the eleventh verse of Matthew 5: "Blessed are *you* when men revile you. . . ." A less common, but quite effec-

tive figure is *climax*, where the thought is emphasized or clarified and given an emotional twist as if by climbing a ladder
(the term means "ladder" in Greek): "We rejoice in our sufferings, knowing that suffering produces endurance, and endurance produces character, and character produces hope, and
hope does not disappoint us" (Rom. 5:3–4).

The theory of figures is more chaotic than most parts of
classical rhetoric. Most figures have both a Greek and a Latin
name, but different authorities use different names for the
same figure, and often they do not agree whether a figure is
one of speech or of thought. Lausberg's *Handbuch* is probably
the best modern source on the terminology, and students may
wish also to consult Ernest W. Bullinger's handbook, *Figures of
Speech Used in the Bible*. Given the name of the figure, it is
relatively easy to find a definition of it in such works or in the
Rhetoric to Herennius or elsewhere in ancient treatises, but
given a passage in which manipulation of words or thought
seems obvious, it is often very difficult to arrive at the appropriate technical description. In addition, a few devices commonly found in ancient texts and given labels by modern critics are not identified at all in handbooks of the classical period.
Chiasmus, or "crossing," is an example. The term appears first
in Pseudo-Hermogenes, *On Invention* (4.3, p. 182 Rabe), a
work perhaps of the fourth century of the Christian era, where
it is applied to a reversed arrangement of clauses in a sentence.
Yet as a figure it is not uncommon in classical Greek literature,
and very common in Latin. The closest parallel term in Latin is
probably *commutatio* (*Rhetoric to Herennius* 4.30), which, to
judge from the examples given, could be applied to such Biblical instances as "The Sabbath was made for man, not man for
the Sabbath" (Mark 2:27). But *commutatio* does not include
everything known as chiasmus. In the Old Testament whole
passages are often composed chiastically, with the parts arranged in a sequence A, B, C, . . . C', B', A'. This elaborated
chiasmus can also be found as a compositional technique in
Greek as early as Homer and is again very common in Latin

poetry of the Augustan period, but it is ignored by classical rhetoricians and literary critics alike.

The Sicilian Jew Caecilius defined a figure as a form of thought or diction not in accordance with nature. Presumably he thought that the only really natural expression is a simple subject-predicate indicative statement, and that any extension, abbreviation, or alteration of this would thus constitute figuring (*schema* in Greek). Figures in the abstract do not have single definable effects; the impact has to be determined from the context. Many are primarily devices of emphasis which call attention to a phrase within a sentence; some, like rhetorical question, help to maintain audience contact. In the New Testament, figures are functional devices, integral to the purpose of the speaker or writer in portraying character, in supporting an argument, or in inducing pathos. There is a valuable discussion of the relation between figures and argument in what is perhaps the most influential modern treatise on rhetoric, *The New Rhetoric* by Chaim Perelman and L. Olbrechts-Tyteca (pp. 167–79).

Figures of thought are especially valuable in the amplification of the basic ideas or topics of a speaker or writer. The *Rhetoric to Herennius* (4.47–69) gives numerous examples to show how this was done in exercises in the rhetorical schools of the early first century before the Christian era. One of the figures discussed is *expolitio*, "refining." *Expolitio* occurs, the author says (4.54), "when we linger on the same topic and seem to be saying something different. It occurs in two forms: we either state the same thing again or we speak about the same thing. We will not say the same thing in the same way— for that would tire the reader, not refine the subject—but you [sic] should change it. We can change it in three ways: by changing the words, by changing the tone of delivery, or by treatment." *Expolitio* is not really a figure at all and is not so regarded by other authorities; it is a technique of amplification, and its closest Greek equivalent is probably *ergasia*, "working out." In refining the "treatment" the author suggests recasting a passage as dialogue or as a rhetorical question revealing personal emotion. The questions asked of Jesus in John 14 are instances of the dialogue treatment inserted into a discourse, for they are refinements of the topics with which Jesus deals. We will examine this in Chapter 3.

In addition to figures, the theory of composition included study of the grouping of phrases and clauses (*commata* and *cola*) into complex sentences or *periods*, as well as the use of rhythms based on the metrical quantities of spoken classical Greek. The definition of what is meant by a period differs somewhat at different times in antiquity, but in modern usage the term usually refers to a complex sentence in which grammatical completion is postponed to the end or almost to the end. How a period in the New Testament can be analyzed into cola and commata is well illustrated in Saint Augustine's discussion of 2 Corinthians 11:16–30 (*On Christian Doctrine* 4.13). Periodic sentences are common in the epistles (the first four verses of Hebrews is the most famous example) but rare in the Gospels other than in Luke. When composition is not periodic, classical critics describe it as in the "running" style. The terms *hypotactic*, or characterized by grammatical subordination, and *paratactic*, characterized by grammatical parallelism, are also sometimes now used to distinguish the periodic and running styles, respectively. Prose rhythms have relatively little role in the rhetorical criticism of the New Testament, the reason being that evidence from inscriptions and papyri seems to indicate that long and short syllables were often not accurately and systematically differentiated in the pronunciation of koine Greek.

Though classical rhetorical theory was developed as a system to teach students how to speak in public, and found its fullest development in formal oratory, it was also utilized to teach and to analyze literary composition. To what extent is an awareness of the conventions of different literary forms essential for valid rhetorical criticism? The answer seems to be that it can be helpful, but that it is not fundamental. Any discourse may be classified as judicial, deliberative, or epideictic and will have the rhetorical characteristics of its species. The inventional techniques of all genres utilize ethos, logos, and pathos. Most principles of arrangement and of style can be found in many different literary forms. An awareness of genre (*genos*) may, however, contribute to an understanding of the rhetorical situation, especially the author's perception of his audience, and it may explain the presence of various features in the work, such as prosopopoeia or the use of apostrophe or dialogue.

Literary categories of genre were developed by grammarians in the Hellenistic period, especially at Alexandria, and were applied primarily to poetry. They are mentioned by rhetoricians chiefly in relation to the training of an orator. Quintilian devotes the first chapter of his tenth book, which is part of his discussion of style, to the works an orator should read to develop *copia*, or "abundance," of thoughts and especially of words. He thinks something can be learned from reading any of the classical writers and in the second chapter of the book continues with a discussion of *mimesis*, or "imitation," which had come to be regarded as the soundest basis for achieving literary excellence. Quintilian regards only three prose genres as literary: oratory, historiography, and the philosophical dialogue, a view which can be found also in Cicero, Dionysius of Halicarnassus, and most other writers. The rhetoricians were aware of the existence of traditional conventions in other forms of composition (in the epistle, for example) but appear to regard these as either subliterary or perhaps more accurately as attaining what literary qualities they have by imitation of one of the three literary genres. Demetrius (223) quotes Artemon, the editor of Aristotle's letters, to the effect that a letter is one of the two sides of a dialogue.

The theory of imitation is part of a general classicizing movement which grammarians and rhetoricians embraced in reaction to a perceived deterioration of prose style in the Hellenistic period. Two opposed phenomena may be distin-

32 RHETORICAL CRITICISM

guished: Asianism and the koine. Asianism is a highly artificial, self-conscious search for striking expression in diction, sentence structure, and rhythm. It deliberately goes to almost any possible extreme. Koine, in contrast, is neither artificial nor very self-conscious and results from the use of Greek as a medium of communication throughout the Near East by persons without deep roots in Greek culture. In contrast to both, grammarians and rhetoricians sought to teach Atticism, which is the use of Greek literary prose of the fifth and fourth centuries before Christ as models for imitation in diction and composition.

One result of these developments was that a writer was now supplied with a possible choice of stylistic registers within varying degrees of Asianism, Atticism, and koine. Examples of all three can be found among early Christian writers, and choice among them seems to reflect, in addition of course to the writer's own education and literary abilities, his perception of his function, his subject, and the audience he intends to reach. Luke and Paul probably could have written Attic Greek if they had wished to, and the apologists of the second century actually do so; Melito of Sardis is even an Asianist. The greater the degree of Atticism, with its classicizing models, the greater the influence of imitation and thus the greater the sense of genre an author is likely to have felt.

Matthew, Mark, and John do not show much awareness of classical literary genres, not even of biography as a nonliterary form with some traditions of its own, derived in part from epideictic oratory through the encomium, in part from the historical monograph (Tacitus' *Life of Agricola*, published in A.D. 98, is a good example of the combination). But the Gospel of Luke shows some awareness of historiography in its use of prosopopoeia and of biography in its treatment of Jesus' youth, and Acts is strongly influenced by the conventions of historiography. Though the New Testament epistles observe conventions such as the salutation, it may be a mistake to try to classify individual epistles within a traditional scheme of classical letter forms, as remarks on Galatians in Chapter 7 below should demonstrate. The influence of the diatribe, also a complex matter, is best left until the discussion of Romans, also in Chapter 7. In general, identification of genre is not a crucial factor in understanding how rhetoric actually works in units of the New Testament.

From this somewhat theoretical background we may turn now to the various stages involved in the practice of rhetorical criticism. These stages are set forth below as a sequence, but it is better to view them as a circular process, for the detailed analysis of later stages may in fact reveal aspects of the rhetorical problem or a definition of the species or stasis which was not obvious on first approaching a passage.

First comes a determination of the *rhetorical unit* to be studied, corresponding to the pericope in form criticism. A rhetorical unit must have a beginning, a middle, and an end. In some cases the determination of the unit is obvious: a speech attributed to Peter or Paul in Acts is clearly intended as a rhetorical unit. Even if the apostle said more at the time, the text is what we have to go on, and the primary objective of rhetorical criticism is to understand the effect of the text. It is doubtless desirable to preserve an awareness of the possible sources of the text, but the determination of those sources is not a primary goal of the method and will not necessarily reveal much about the qualities of the finished product. When the rhetorical unit, such as a speech, is contained within a larger unit, in this case the Acts of the Apostles, we may need an awareness of the overall rhetoric of the book (for example, the extent to which its author intended to conform to some conventions of Greek historiography or wished to minimize the existence of dissension in the early Church), but the rhetoric of large units often has to be built up from an understanding of the rhetoric of smaller units. In the case of the short epistles of the New Testament it is possible to begin with the whole letter as a unit. The most difficult cases involve portions of longer works which are not immediately evident self-contained units, as is a speech. Here we must experiment by seeking signs of opening and closure (for which the term *inclusio* is sometimes used), of proem and epilogue. Of course, we must not rely on chapter divisions, since they are the work of later editors and not a part of the original text. Often the paragraphing of modern editions and translations will be found rhetorically faulty. Fortunately, the narrative technique of the Bible, both Old and New Testaments, often makes use of closures. Someone begins to do something and engages in various acts or in dialogue; this is described; the author then returns to the original situation, sometimes even summing up what has been described in a single verse: "And he went away and began to proclaim in the Decapolis how much Jesus had done for him; and all men marveled" (Mark 5:20). This constitutes closure of a rhetorical unit. One rhetorical unit may be enclosed within another, building up a structure which embraces the whole book. In rhetorical criticism it is important that the rhetorical unit chosen have some magnitude. It has to have within itself a discernible beginning and ending, connected by some action or argument. Five or six verses probably constitute the minimum text which can be subjected to rhetorical criticism as a distinct unit, but most will be longer, extending for the better part of a chapter or for several chapters.

Once a preliminary determination of the rhetorical unit has been made, the critic should attempt to define the *rhetorical situation* of the unit. This roughly corresponds to the *Sitz im Leben* of form criticism. The concept of rhetorical situation was first promulgated by Lloyd F. Bitzer. Although theoretical objections have been raised to his original formation, it proves a useful tool of practical criticism. Bitzer points out (pp. 4–6) that "a particular discourse comes into existence because of some specific condition or situation which invites utterance. The situation controls the rhetorical response in the same sense that the question controls the answer and the problem controls the solution." He defines rhetorical situation as "a complex of persons, events, objects, and relations presenting an actual or potential exigence which can be completely or partially removed if discourse, introduced into the situation, can so constrain human decision or action as to bring about the significant modification of the exigence." What Bitzer means by an "exigence" is a situation under which an individual is called upon to make some response: the response made is conditioned by the situation and in turn has some possibility of affecting the situation or what follows from it. A common example is a defendant brought before a judge; the defendant may be able to answer the charge. But the exigence may not be so immediate and need not be oral. The reports which reached Paul of the situation in Corinth seemed to him to require a response; the result is 1 Corinthians. In a still broader way we may say that an evangelist felt an exigence to proclaim the gospel, and that in doing so he felt an exigence to include certain of the doings or sayings of Jesus which reveal that gospel or help to establish its validity.

The aspects of situation which Bitzer suggests the rhetorical critic should examine are the persons, events, objects, and relations involved. They influence what is said and why. In logic these factors are known as *categories*, and they supply the basis for the inventional topics employed in the rhetorical unit. Additional categories include time and place. Among the persons involved, the most important are often those who make up the audience. The critic needs to ask of what this audience consists, what the audience expects in the situation, and how the speaker or writer manipulates these expectations. There may be both an immediate and a universal audience, especially in a written work. The Gospel of Luke is immediately addressed to Theophilus but surely intended for a wider readership. In an influential passage of the *Phaedrus* (271a) Plato asserts that a true philosophical orator must know the souls of his audience. Aristotle sought to give this practical application by considering audience in terms of categories of age and worldly estate: a speech addressed to the young will have different rhetorical qualities from one addressed to the old; a speech to the rich (like Clement of Alexandria's homily "What rich man is saved?") will differ from a speech to the poor (the poor in spirit and the meek of the Sermon on the Mount).

In many rhetorical situations the speaker will be found to face one overriding *rhetorical problem*. His audience is perhaps already prejudiced against him and not disposed to listen to anything he may say; or the audience may not perceive him as having the authority to advance the claims he wishes to make; or what he wishes to say is very complicated and thus hard to follow, or so totally different from what the audience expects that they will not immediately entertain the possibility of its truth. This problem is often especially visible at the beginning of a discourse and conditions the contents of the proem or the beginning of the proof. Classical rhetoricians developed a technique of approaching a difficult rhetorical problem indirectly, known as *insinuatio* (see *Rhetoric to Herennius* 1.9–11). The problem may color the treatment throughout the speech, and sometimes a speaker is best advised to lay a foundation for understanding on the part of the audience before bringing up the central problem.

Two other parts of classical theory which are useful in a preliminary approach to the rhetorical unit are *stasis theory* and the theory of the three *species of rhetoric*. Stasis theory is exceedingly complex, and discussion of it probably should not be undertaken by a student before extensive reading in the rhetorical sources. Determination of the species, as the discussion of Galatians in Chapter 7 below reveals, can be crucial in understanding the unit. As outlined above in the survey of rhetorical theory, the three species are judicial, which seeks to bring about a judgment about events of the past; deliberative, which aims at effecting a decision about future action, often in the very immediate future; and epideictic, which celebrates or condemns someone or something, not seeking an immediate judgment or action, but increasing or undermining assent to some value. Each has characteristic features; in deliberative, for example, there is often a preponderance of inductive argument based on past example, along with emphasis on the advantages to be obtained from some course of action. The audience in a deliberative occasion is often directly involved in the matter, and the speaker needs to do less to interest them than he might do to secure a favorable judgment for himself or some other person as a result of past actions.

After these considerations of preliminary matters the rhetorical critic is prepared to proceed to consider the *arrangement of material* in the text: what subdivisions it falls into, what the persuasive effect of these parts seems to be, and how they work together—or fail to do so—to some unified purpose in meeting the rhetorical situation. In order to do this he will need to engage in line-by-line analysis of the argument, including its assumptions, its topics, and its formal features, such as enthymemes, and of the *devices of style*, seeking to define their function in context. This process will reveal how the raw material has been worked out or rhetorically amplified both in context and in style. It should be kept in mind that a speech or a text read aloud is presented linearly: the audience hears the words in progression without opportunity to review what has been said earlier, and an orally received text is characterized by a greater degree of repetition than is a text intended to be read privately. The New Testament was intended to be received orally and abounds in repetition. It should also be kept in mind, however, that many reports of discourse in the New Testament are too short for their actual occasion. In Mark 6:34–35 and Luke 9:12 Jesus seems to have been speaking for an extended period of time, and we know that Saint Paul once preached until midnight (Acts 20:7) and on another occasion from morning until evening (Acts 28:23). Only a few speeches in the New Testament, the Sermon on the Mount and the defense of Stephen, for example, are extensive enough to represent an entire speech without compression or abbreviation. Sometimes the text itself reveals that some selection has been made. Finally, some speeches in the New Testament must be regarded as prosopopoeiae, inventions of a writer on the basis of what a speaker probably would have said, analogues to the speeches in Greek historians. It seems unlikely that Luke knew exactly what the angel said to the Virgin Mary and how she expressed her joy (1:26–56) or what words Zechariah used in his prophecy (1:67–80). Discourses attributed to Jesus and the speeches in Acts are special cases to be considered later.

At the end of the process of analysis it will be valuable to look back over the entire unit and review its success in meeting the rhetorical exigence and what its implications may be for the speaker or audience. Is the detailed analysis consistent with the overall impact of the rhetorical unit? Has attention to the trees somehow obscured a view of the woods? Rhetorical and literary composition are creative acts: the whole is often greater than the sum of the parts, at least the parts as coldly analyzed. Criticism too can be a creative act, not only bringing the target text into clearer focus, but looking beyond it to an awareness of the human condition, of the economy and beauty of discourse, and to religious or philosophical truth.

From the theory of rhetorical criticism we may now proceed to experiment with its practice. The discussions which follow are not intended as authoritative, final expositions of the rhetoric of the New Testament, but as examples of how one might go about analyzing it and what kind of results might ensue.

Chapter Two. Deliberative Rhetoric: The Sermon on the Mount, the Sermon on the Plain, and the Rhetoric of Jesus

The fifth, sixth, and seventh chapters of the Gospel of Matthew and the sixth chapter of the Gospel of Luke present sermons attributed to Jesus early in his ministry. Many, perhaps most, modern biblical scholars, working with the tools of form and redaction criticism, regard these as the work of the evangelists editing traditional material into the form of continuous speeches. The question of the sources and authenticity of the speeches is an interesting one on which a few comments may be made later, but it is irrelevant to the question of how the Gospels should be read. It was the intent of the evangelists to present speeches, and early Christian audiences, listening to the Gospels read, heard these chapters as speeches. In applying rhetorical criticism, we may initially claim no more than to be examining the rhetoric of the evangelists and seeking to see how the chapters work within an understanding of classical rhetoric.

In accordance with the method outlined in Chapter 1 above, we begin by determining the *rhetorical unit* of the Sermon on the Mount. This is specified in the text: Matthew 5:2, "And *he opened his mouth* and taught them, saying . . ." to 7:28, "And *when Jesus finished* these sayings, the crowds were astonished at his teaching, for he taught them as one who had authority and not as their scribes." It is thus Matthew's clear intention that we regard this as a complete speech: no words follow it and no interruption is noted during the speech.

In Chapter 4 Matthew provides information about the *rhetorical situation* which he wishes readers to envision. Jesus, early in his ministry, has been traveling through Galilee teaching in synagogues, but this speech is not set in a synagogue; it is set out of doors on a hill in the presence of a much larger crowd than could be assembled in a synagogue. A majority of the crowd may be Galileans, but we are told that there are also present people from the Decapolis, Jerusalem, Judea, and beyond the Jordan (4:25). These people have been attracted to Jesus in the first instance as a healer: "So his fame spread throughout all Syria, and they brought him all the sick, those afflicted with various diseases and pains, demoniacs, epileptics, and paralytics, and he healed them" (4:24). Some in the audience may be regarded as familiar with the teachings of John the Baptist and as thinking of Jesus as the Messiah; Jesus' claim in 5:17 that he comes to fulfill the law and the prophets would be meaningful to this group and would contribute to his authority in the speech. Matthew probably wants readers to assume that word of Jesus' teaching in the synagogues had spread and that some in the crowd have come to find out what he teaches as well as to see if he can heal.

It has been assumed by some commentators, at least since the time of John Chrysostom, that the sermon is primarily addressed to the disciples and only secondarily to others. The textual basis for this conclusion is the "them" (*autous*) of 5:2, for which the closest grammatical antecedent is the "disciples" of 5:1. But this interpretation must be set against the "them" of 7:28 in the closure of the speech, "for he taught them as one having authority," where "them" grammatically can only refer to the crowd as a whole. "Them" in 5:2 can in fact also refer to the crowd, which is mentioned in 5:1. This interpretation is confirmed by 7:24, "everyone then who hears these words." That the entire crowd constitutes the audience is further supported by the various categories of people mentioned in the Beatitudes and throughout: the poor, the grief-stricken, the meek, those contemplating divorce, all Jews who will pray.

In Luke 6:20, on the plain, Jesus first raises his eyes to the disciples and then begins to speak, employing the second person plural as early as the first beatitude; again the second person cannot be easily limited to the disciples. In most rhetorical situations there is a formal addressee, for example a chairman in a meeting, who is nominally addressed, though practically speaking the speaker is addressing all those present and sometimes turns directly to them. In classical oratory, apostrophe, or the turn from the nominal addressee to someone else, is even more common than in modern public address. What perhaps should be envisioned in Matthew, as in Luke, is that Jesus first looks at the disciples and then begins to refer to the crowd in the third person, shifting abruptly to the second person in 5:11. This verse may be addressed directly to the disciples, since they alone at this point can be assumed to be committed to the gospel, but beginning with 5:13 and continuing throughout the sermon the reference of the second person is enlarged to include the entire crowd, as 7:28 makes clear. The point is of some theological significance in determining whether Matthew thought the teachings he has attributed to Jesus were to be followed only by a small group, committed to the religious life as are the disciples or religious orders of later times, or whether the sermon is addressed to all who hear him. The rhetorical situation suggests that Jesus is to be regarded as beginning by addressing the disciples, but changing to an address to the crowd. They are amazed at what he says: his message is new to them, but they instinctively feel his authority (7:28). We will need to consider how that authority is established in the text. The disciples have heard something of the message before in the synagogues and show no surprise.

The interpretation just advanced raises a recurring problem of possible conflicts between results of form or redaction criticism and rhetorical criticism. Some scholars are likely to reply that passages in the second person plural reveal the use of a common source, often called *Q*, by Matthew and Luke and that variations in the person in Matthew's text of the sermon are thus not necessarily deliberate or significant, except as signs of his source. But we are seeking to describe what Muilenberg,

quoted in Chapter 1 above, called "the creative synthesis of the
particular formation of the pericope." That synthesis was what
the writer felt was "right," a complex combination of historically right, theologically right, and rhetorically right. Matthew
clearly wished the sermon to be perceived as a speech; he had a
good ear for rhetoric, as should become clearer in Chapter 5
below. He was surely not deliberately leaving his readers clues
to unravel his use of sources. In his choice, combination, and
editing of sources he engaged in a deliberate process, though
not necessarily a consciously deliberate process. Apostrophe
and other changes of person were a regular feature of public
address in his times, and he could not escape some ear for
them. When an early Christian audience heard his Gospel they
recognized those changes in addressee, and they would have
felt them as part of the internal dynamics of the speech, not as
clues to Matthew's sources. A doctrinaire insistence on source
criticism tends to underestimate Matthew's abilities as a writer
and the perceptual sensitivity of his intended audience; rhetorical criticism can help to redress that estimate.

Matthew shows Jesus confronting a large and varied crowd,
drawn to him primarily for personal and physical reasons,
knowing little about him or his message. They are, however,
sympathetic or at least not hostile: some have already been
healed or witnessed healing; others hope to be healed, as apparently happens after the sermon (8:1–4). There is no evidence in Matthew's description of the situation, as contrasted
to Luke's, to indicate that the audience includes members of
Jewish sects hostile to Jesus and his teachings as violations of
law, but it is of course still early in his ministry. Jesus is shown
to anticipate such hostility in his words in 5:11. His success as a
healer is the first basis of his authority. Throughout the Bible,
miracles, of which healing is the most personal form, together
with the fulfillment of the prophecies of the Old Testament
and witnesses, constitute the external proof. Here they are
totally external to Jesus' sermon: he never refers to them in the
text.

What *exigence*, then, as described in the critical method outlined in Chapter 1, does the rhetorical situation provide? Those present ask no question and would probably be content if Jesus passed among them, healing the sick. The exigence must be assumed to originate with Jesus, with his understanding of his mission and his anticipation of its effect. First, he has something to do, of which healing is only a preliminary part. He has a message to proclaim and is looking for opportunities to proclaim it, either in synagogues or in public meetings. That Matthew thinks of Jesus as a teacher is indicated by his mentioning that Jesus delivers his sermon seated (5:1), even though he would doubtless have been more visible standing and might have had more worldly authority. Worldly authority he does not seek; he wants the traditional authority of a Jewish teacher. An audience would probably sense the difference. The disciples, we are told, sat around Jesus. In the Greco-Roman world, as in many cultures including our own, it was customary for a public speaker to be escorted and thus supported by his friends. Jesus may not have needed moral support, but the disciples' location helps to sustain his message, for they thus affirm their acceptance of it. In rhetorical terms they are his witnesses, part of his external proof. This effect would be increased in the minds of anyone in the crowd who knew or thought well of the disciples or—since they were not well-known people—had been impressed by their compassion as they moved among the crowd in advance of the speech.

A second exigence is suggested by Jesus' remarks in 5:11 and is a key to a *rhetorical problem* he faces: "Blessed are you when men revile you and persecute you and utter all kinds of evil against you falsely on my account." He wishes to prepare the disciples and others who may follow him for subsequent encounters with opposition. His thesis is that he came "not to abolish the law and the prophets, but to fulfill them" (5:17). Anticipation of objections, known in classical rhetoric as *prokatalepsis*, is a feature of a great deal of oratory. It has to be handled with some care, for it may seem to throw the orator on the defensive and undermine his credibility, especially if he seems to acknowledge strong arguments against him and does not answer them with absolute conviction. Jesus is shown avoiding this pitfall by his confident authority and by presenting his view of the law in a positive way without specifying how he may be thought to contravene it.

What has been said so far relates to the exigence experienced by Jesus as portrayed by Matthew. It might also be asked what is the exigence experienced by Matthew. Why, in contrast to Mark, does he feel the need to attribute a speech to Jesus here, perhaps even to construct one out of a collection of Jesus' sayings? A satisfactory answer to that question involves an overall awareness of Matthew's rhetoric, about which something will be said in Chapter 5, but some factors may be mentioned here. The evangelists, including Mark, knew traditions of Jesus' preaching in synagogues and elsewhere. Because the gospel accounts were amplified from whatever sources were available, including the evangelists' own sense of inspiration, some report of this preaching would fill an obvious gap in the record and would interest an audience. Matthew writes for an intelligent audience of some education, at least within the Jewish tradition. Given the society of the Greek-speaking world in the first century, both Matthew and his audience held certain assumptions about communication. One was that the ordinary form of presentation of important ideas was through continuous discourse, orally presented. Even the Old Testament makes great use of speeches, and the Greeks had elevated public address into the central feature of civilized life. For such an audience it was important to include a speech of Jesus. A second assumption was that such a speech should come early in a work, where it could perform some of the functions of a rhetorical proposition. The entire thrust of Greek education in grammar, rhetoric, and dialectic was in the direction of encouraging a statement of a thesis to be followed by its proof, illustration, and application. As will be shown in Chapter 5, Matthew felt an exigence to supply a Gospel which would be intellectually satisfying in a way that Mark's Gospel was not. The Sermon on the Mount helps to fill that need.

It might be thought that the radical and even paradoxical

nature of Jesus' teaching would constitute a rhetorical problem for Matthew. That would perhaps have been the case before an audience of Pharisees and might have been the case when speaking in a synagogue. In such situations Jesus is usually shown as stressing fulfillment of prophecies of Scripture. Here, conversely, little is said about prophecy, and the paradox of the Beatitudes and the radical teaching on the law become assets in getting the attention and the sympathy of an audience which had little to lose and thought it had little to hope.

The sermon as a whole is deliberative: Jesus gives advice, quite specific advice, on the conduct of life. He looks to the immediate future. For those who had been healed, or were soon to be healed, a new future life was now opening, and doubtless for many of their relatives as well. He invites them to consider how they are going to live that new life, and the advice he gives is new to them. If the sermon is read with this in mind, the contrast maintained throughout between the law as understood in the past and as Jesus understands it is given a new and more personal force. The Beatitudes are epideictic elements in that they celebrate qualities, but their position at the beginning of the speech requires that they function as a proem; they would certainly so be perceived by an audience in New Testament times. A proem regularly shows epideictic traits. There is no marked judicial element in the sermon, no judgment of the past, either applied to the Jews as a whole or to individuals, though certain classes of individuals in the present are referred to negatively: tax collectors, hypocrites, and gentiles. It is a regular technique of skilled orators to suggest solidarity between themselves and their audience by playing upon a common hostility to others, sometimes even setting up straw men. As has been said, the sermon is not addressed to a small group of disciples, but neither in its context is it addressed to all men and women of all time. It is addressed to the "lost sheep of the house of Israel" (10:6), the people of an exploited client kingdom of the Roman empire, and doubtless to be understood in the eschatological terms made explicit in Matthew 10. Albert Schweitzer's conception that the teaching of the sermon is interim ethics, though not proved, is in no way contradicted by the rhetoric of the speech.

The focus of argument in deliberative rhetoric is self-interest and the expedient: not necessarily unenlightened and not dishonorable self-interest, but self-interest. This is clearly true of the Sermon on the Mount. Jesus actually uses the words *sympherei soi*, "it is expedient for you" (5:29, 30), which are characteristic of classical deliberative oratory. The focus of argument is clearly brought out again by the end of the speech: "Everyone who hears these words of mine and does them will be like a wise man, . . . everyone who hears these words of mine and does not do them will be like a foolish man who built his house upon the sand" (7:24). The reward will be personal, and probably soon.

Classical critics thought that *stasis theory* was applicable to deliberative rhetoric, even though its categories were largely developed for use in the lawcourts. The stasis here would seem to be primarily stasis of fact: *what* should be done and by whom. That is what most of the sermon is about, and that is how it ends. The anticipation of the objection that Jesus has come to abolish the law makes some use of that part of stasis theory which deals with legal questions, since there is an implied contrast between the word and intent of the law, or an extension of the law to apply to situations not specifically covered. Though Jesus may be said to show interest in the quality of life of his audience, that quality is to be a result of specific actions, and not of attitude, motivation, or attendant circumstances, which are characteristic of stasis of quality. This again has a theological implication: salvation, as taught in the Sermon on the Mount, comes not from faith, but from works. Jesus conspicuously refrains from saying what he points out in other contexts: that it is the audience's faith that has made or will make them whole. A passage which may imply faith begins at 7:7: "Ask, and it will be given you; seek, and you will find." But this very passage ends with the rule of expediency: "Whatever you wish that men do to you, do so to them" (7:12). Its negative version, open to fewer moral objections, is found in Romans 13:10 and elsewhere, but would be inappropriate to Jesus' emphasis here on action. The absence of much emphasis on faith can probably, on rhetorical grounds, be linked to the occasion, for which it is hardly necessary. The crowd has seen the miracles, they already have an openness to faith and need not nurture it in contemplation, for the kingdom soon will come.

This interpretation may seem inconsistent with the reading of the sermon by commentators who find in the Beatitudes an unstated agenda, an intent to show that no one can possibly, by works alone, live up to the teaching that follows, and thus to assert a doctrine of grace. The problem is a complex one, and the crucial factors in interpretation are the perception of the rhetorical unit and the identification of the audience. Taking Matthew 5–7 as the rhetorical unit, which Matthew asks us to do, and inquiring how an early Christian audience would understand the sermon, the answer has to be that it preaches works, not faith. This is because of the principle of linearity. The audience's attention is drawn from the initial appeal of the Beatitudes, through the specific commandments, to the demand that they be obeyed. That is where the audience is left. A doctrine of grace can be attributed to the speech by approaching it as a literary product, that is, by returning to the Beatitudes after reading through the chapters and treating them not as a proem, but as a separate discourse deliberately set back-to-back with what follows, to challenge a reader. This requires considerable sophistication on the part of the audience: not just a willingness to receive an oral text at its face value, but an insistence on asking questions about it and relating it to what Jesus says on other occasions. The result is to regard the bulk of the sermon as ironic. Irony is a rhetorical convention of the Greco-Roman world, but not on this scale, at least not in speeches, and Matthew's audience can hardly be expected to have appreciated such irony.

The Sermon on the Mount, read as a speech in its context in the Gospel of Matthew, is important evidence of how Matthew perceived Jesus' public teaching early in his ministry. The

rhetorical critic can point out to the theologian how the sermon would have been perceived; it is then the theologian's
task to utilize that evidence in building an interpretation of the
ministry of Jesus or of Christian doctrine as a whole. A possible explanation is that Matthew did not understand Jesus, just
as Xenophon sometimes did not understand the irony of Socrates. Another type of explanation, commonly used by scholars
in the interpretation of apparent inconsistencies in the work of
other teachers (for example, Plato or Aristotle) is that their
doctrines evolved over time or that there was a difference between their doctrines as expounded to their close followers and
to the wider public. The latter at least seems a possible approach in the case of Jesus.

When a deliberative orator needs to attract the attention and
acquire the goodwill of an audience as Jesus does—and in
some deliberative situations that is not necessary—he begins
with a formal proem. This is conventionally followed by the
proposition, proposal, or thesis of the speaker, and then evidence to support his view. Sometimes narrative is required,
sometimes related issues are taken up, sometimes a previous
speaker is refuted. Greek rhetoricians of the Roman period
refer to this central body of a speech as the "headings" (*kepha-
laia*) since the orator often groups his arguments to demonstrate that the action he supports is possible and that it will be
expedient, or just, or honorable, or consistent with the values
of the audience, or the only possible course of action. At the
end of a speech there is commonly an epilogue; in classical
theory its primary functions are to recapitulate the points the
speaker has made and to arouse the emotions of the audience
toward action, but in a short speech recapitulation may not be
necessary and a coolly rational summary may be inimical to the
orator's objective. Greek oratory, as seen for example in the
speeches of Demosthenes, tends to reach its emotional climax
near the middle of a speech and end quietly and thoughtfully;
Roman oratory, as seen in Cicero, is more often passionate at
the end.

In the Sermon on the Mount, Matthew 5:17–20 can be said

to assert the basic proposition: Jesus has come to fulfill the law; even the least of its commandments must be observed, and one must go beyond these commandments as understood by contemporary religious authorities. Whatever precedes the proposition, in this case Matthew 5:3–16, would be perceived as the proem. Jesus' injunctions and supporting evidence end with the passage warning against false prophets in 7:15–20. What follows that, 7:21–27, may be rhetorically viewed as the epilogue: 7:21–23 is recapitulatory, followed by pathetic appeal. These then constitute the three major rhetorical divisions of the sermon: proem, proposition and headings, epilogue. As we look at them in turn it should be remembered that in classical theory there are three and only three internal modes of persuasion: ethos (authority and character), logos (inductive and deductive argument), and pathos (emotional appeal).

The various categories of people mentioned in the Beatitudes are those with which Jesus' audience can easily and immediately identify. Some would regard themselves as merciful, perhaps with little other claim to virtue; many doubtless sought to be pure of heart, some had sought to be peacemakers, some had experienced persecution or oppression or exploitation. These overlapping groups are the people whose interest and goodwill Jesus wishes to secure. Each of the Beatitudes constitutes an enthymeme. The conclusion is given first (for example, "Blessed are the poor in spirit"), then a supporting reason, introduced by *hoti* in Greek or "for" in English translations. An enthymeme characteristically omits or suppresses one of its premises. In this case the major premise is tacitly assumed: "All who will obtain the kingdom of heaven are blessed." The clauses introduced by "for" are the minor premises: "The poor in spirit will obtain the kingdom of heaven." Therefore, conclusion, "The poor in spirit are blessed." Each of the Beatitudes can be restated in a similar manner. For example, those who will obtain mercy are blessed; the merciful will obtain mercy; therefore the merciful are blessed. The Beatitudes take enthymematic, and thus syllogistic form, and are *formally* valid. Formal validity helps to make them acceptable to the audience, for Jesus thus seems to give a reason why anyone in any of these groups should regard himself as blessed; but whether or not the logic is wholly valid is also dependent on the validity of the premises. The implied major premise (for example, "All who will obtain the kingdom of heaven are blessed") is categorical and constitutes a definition; it can be said to lie in the area of a commonly acceptable definition. Its chief logical problems are whether the certainty of a future state can be used as a predicate for a condition in the present, and what constitutes the kingdom of heaven. In the Greek text no word for "are" is expressed: Jesus says, as he would have in Aramaic, "Blessed the poor in spirit!"—avoiding the first logical problem. The kingdom of heaven probably had meaning to his audience; at the very least it was regarded as a good thing. An orator has a right to make his own definitions on the basis of what is commonly believed or acceptable.

The validity of the minor premises ("The poor in spirit will obtain the kingdom of heaven," and so forth) is more dubious. Their acceptability to Jesus' audience was based on the fact that he said them, and on the audience's will to believe. In other words, the value of these premises is dependent on all three factors in the speech situation: speaker, speech, and audience. Jesus speaks with external authority, based on the miracles he has performed, strengthened by his general reputation, his role as rabbi and perhaps Messiah, and the support of the disciples. He seeks to make the minor premises more acceptable to his audience by avoiding any attempt to justify them, thus relying on the ethos of his authority, and also by the way he puts the verbs into the future tense. Whereas the tense constitutes a logical problem in the case of the implied major premises, the future facilitates the acceptance of the minor premises: an objective observer might not believe that these people *are* blessed, but it would be difficult to prove that none of them *will* inherit the kingdom of heaven. (It might be noted that Greek does not distinguish between "shall" and "will" as does English, and the common translations "shall be comforted," "shall inherit the earth" are a rhetorical emphasis added to the text by English translators perhaps justified by the demonstrative pronoun *autoi* in the Greek.) The future orientation of the Beatitudes is of course important as part of the deliberative nature of Jesus' sermon and of his eschatological views, but it is also an important ingredient in their emotional appeal, or pathos. The audience wants to believe what is being told them so confidently, wants to feel that there is some worthiness in each of them which will be rewarded in the future. A rhetorician might say that Jesus "plays upon" that feeling; perhaps it would be fairer to say that he understands it and shares it. Finally, it may be noted that the order of the premises encourages persuasion. By putting the conclusion first, a conclusion which the audience would like to believe, the minor premise appears as a reason which seems to offer confirmation.

The form of Jesus' proem as a whole also contributes to the acceptability of what he says. It is probable that the Beatitudes have formal antecedents in Jewish poetry, which may have been known to some in the audience, and thus some familiarity, but they are also arresting, and their parallelism establishes a pattern in which each may be said to contribute to the acceptance of the whole. Each constitutes a period in two cola, but the last is extended (5:12) for three additional cola. The anaphora, or repetition of "blessed," stresses the most appealing word in each. A figure of speech thus becomes a functional device of persuasion. The language is simple, as appropriate to a simple audience, but there are striking metaphors which impart reality to the utterances, especially "inherit the earth" and "see God." Beyond this, paradox, paradoxically, can have a persuasive quality. It alerts the audience and suggests that there is more to be heard than meets the ear. In the Greek text there are additional figures of speech which tie the whole passage together: a tendency toward alliteration of the initial letter *p*; and homoeoteleuton, seen in the rhyming syllables *-esontai* found at the end of five of the Beatitudes and balancing the initial anaphora. Careful analysis might well reveal additional techniques of style, but those listed are adequate to make the point that the words contribute to a unified persuasive effect. The whole passage has a mystical quality arising from terms which are not explained, though some of them had traditional meanings perhaps known to the audience: "kingdom of heaven," "inherit the earth," "called sons of God." Christian rhetoric of late antiquity and the Byzantine period makes extensive use of what is called *emphasis*, a deliberate obscurity in which words are used without specific definitions, implying meanings beyond the power of the human mind to verbalize or define, and this tradition can be traced back to John, to Paul, and to the prophets and beyond.

Rhetorical analysis does not suggest any clear reason why the Beatitudes are arranged in the specific sequence in which we find them here, but the position of certain ones may be said to be rhetorically effective. The first has the advantage of incorporating a reference to the kingdom of heaven in the opening sentence of the sermon. This is perhaps echoed in "inherit the earth" in the third and taken up again in "they shall see God" in the sixth. The theme is maintained in the seventh and eighth, the latter rounding out the sequence with its reference to the kingdom of God. The ninth is distinctly different, characterized by the figure apostrophe, the turn from the third person of the other Beatitudes to address "you when men revile you." We know almost nothing about Jesus' delivery, which is an important part of rhetoric, but it is possible that he here should be imagined as looking at the disciples and, as said above, that "you" refers to them. Certainly they will most directly bear the persecution and their activities will be most parallel to "the prophets who were before you."

Once the second person is introduced in this dramatic way, it is largely maintained throughout the sermon, but, as argued above, broadened to include the whole audience. In "You are the salt of the earth," "You are the light of the world," the second person plural embraces all the groups itemized in the Beatitudes into one unified tribute, but each tribute is accompanied by a warning which lays the groundwork for the preaching which is to follow. It is not simply a matter that the poor in spirit or the meek can sit back and wait: they will be called upon to do good works. Salt can lose its savor and should be used while fresh; a light is no good if under a bushel. Verse 13 is cast as a rhetorical question: "How shall its saltiness be restored?" The implied answer is "It cannot." It can only be thrown out to be trodden underfoot by men. "By men" makes a good contrast with "kingdom of God." The question helps to maintain rapport with the audience; the metaphor, man as salt, as is usually the case with Jesus' examples, is a homely and practical one within everyone's experience. It functions here as an inductive argument, which can, like all inductions, be recast as an enthymeme. Example: salt loses its savor and can only be cast out. Assumption: *other* active substances also lose their effectiveness. Induced general conclusion: any active substance can lose its effectiveness. This then becomes a major premise to which a minor premise can be assumed: man is an active substance. Conclusion: man can lose his effectiveness, like salt. The simile "like salt" is then recast as metaphor: "you are salt." The second comparison, to a light, is treated in the same way, except that it is given greater amplification. Amplification is a rhetorical device whereby a speaker dwells on a thought and thus gives it greater emphasis. Here the light is amplified by being compared to a city and it is not only lit, but put on a stand where the result is specified: it gives light to all in the house. Not to the whole house, but to *all* in the house; the image is thought of in personal terms. The purpose of amplifying the second image is that Jesus wishes to build his conclusion upon it, implicit in the salt image, here explicit: "that they may *see* your good works and give glory to your Father who is in heaven." The word "see" of course carries out the light imagery.

At this point the proem is complete. Jesus, as portrayed by Matthew, has established his relationship to the audience; he has anticipated the possibility of future opposition from outside the group; he has laid the foundation for his message: it is not enough to thirst for righteousness, but good works are demanded. He is now ready to move to his proposition, its implication, and the enthymemes and examples which will support it. The authoritative ethos remains strong, but rational conclusions based on the analogies of everyday life are being employed. So far, pathos has played only an implicit role, evoked by the use of occasional pathetic words in the proem: mourn, comfort, revile, persecute, rejoice, be glad. Each of the experiences of suffering, properly understood, will be converted into an experience of joy.

The primary justification for viewing Matthew 5:17–20 as the proposition of the sermon is that it enunciates, but does not explicate, the two principles which are the basis of much that follows in the speech. These are that the law is to be observed in all its details in future actions of the audience and that their righteousness (*dikaiosyne*) must exceed that of the scribes and Pharisees, the traditional interpreters of the law. Jesus then, starting in 5:21, takes up various injunctions of the law, such as "thou shall not kill," and shows how each is to be interpreted in accordance with this greater "justice." It is characteristic of a proposition in a speech that is asserted confidently. Jesus is thus shown with what is, even for him, a heightened authority of expression: "think not"; "for truly"; "for I tell you". He polarizes the issue: "not an iota, not a dot"; "least in the kingdom" versus "great in the kingdom." The proposition of a speech, even in civic discourse, is not the place to suggest compromise, and here qualities of sacred language come into play as well. Jesus states the first of his premises in verse 17, further strengthens that premise in verse 18, gives a threat and a promise in verse 19, and enunciates the second premise in verse 20. The words "for" (*gar*) in verses 18 and 20 are not signs of enthymemes here, as they often are in other contexts, but particles of emphasis in the two key injunctions of the propositions. Ethos and pathos are stronger here than logos: ethos in Jesus' authority, pathos in the punishment or reward decreed in verse 19. In the rhetorical situation of the sermon, Jesus' power to reward or punish has been exhibited in his healing. The crowd could fear he might withhold the kingdom of heaven. That phrase, "kingdom of heaven," appears twice in emphatic position at the ends of verses 19 and 20 and serves as a reminder of the promises of the Beatitudes.

The headings which follow are developed out of the proposition and are divided into two groups. The first group, which makes up the rest of chapter 5, explains Jesus' view of the principle of the law; the second group begins with the reference to *dikaiosyne* in 6:1 (taking up the term from 5:20 of the proposition) and extends to 6:18. This structure is unfortunately obscured in the Revised Standard Version by translating *dikaiosyne* in 5:20 as "righteousness" and in 6:1 as "piety." The most striking rhetorical difference between the two groups of headings is that those in the first group are supported chiefly by the use of ethos and pathos, whereas those in the second group are more often expressed as enthymemes; they have supporting argument. The heading found in 5:21–26 may be taken as an example of the first group. Like the others, it is built on a strong antithesis: "You have heard that it was said. . . . But I say to you." In the first part of the antithesis the actual words of the law are quoted, giving them scriptural authority; in the second part acceptance of the injunctions depends in the first instance on the ethos of Jesus as we have seen it in the situation and the proem, but this is strengthened by amplification and by pathos. The amplification is seen both in quantity and quality: quantity in that Jesus devotes several verses to elaboration of his injunction, quality in that the tone is heightened by words like "everyone," "whoever," and "the last penny," and also by the figure of thought called climax: "liable to judgment . . . liable to the council . . . liable to the hell of fire"; "hand you over to the judge, and the judge to the guard, and you be put in prison."

Jesus is shown as deadly serious about his extensions of the law, but the rhetoric shows that some of the *examples* he cites are not to be taken literally. In the second heading, that on adultery, the concept of the eye causing one to sin is a metaphor; since that is so, the injunction to cast out the eye and throw it away can also be metaphorically understood. And similarly with the right hand which offends.

The proof of 5:17–48 is largely based on ethos and pathos, not on logical argument, but there are a few exceptions to this observation which deserve to be examined. They are marked by the use of the word "for" (*gar* or *hoti* in Greek). In 5:29, having recommended plucking out the offending eye, Jesus continues, "[for] it is better that you lose one of your members than that your whole body be cast into hell," and a similar clause completes verse 30 on casting away the right hand. The Revised Standard Version omits the "for" (present in the Greek as *gar*), and the translators' instinct is understandable. Formally speaking, 5:29 and 5:30 are enthymemes, employing what Aristotle would call the topic of the more and the less, but the effect of the clauses here seems not so much logical as pathetical; they function as a part of the amplification.

In the heading on oaths occur several clauses introduced in the Greek text by *hoti*, "for" or "because," utilizing wording of the Jewish law: "Do not swear at all either by heaven, for it is the throne of God, or by the earth, for it is his footstool, or by Jerusalem, for it is the city of the great king. And do not swear by your head, for you cannot make one hair white or black" (5:34–36). These all take the form of enthymemes, but it is not clear that they should be viewed as logical arguments. The point of an oath is to affix an action to something which the swearer cannot change. It is possible that the *hoti* clauses should be viewed as the excuse of the *swearer*, not Jesus' argument; thus 5:36 could be paraphrased: "Do not swear by your head, alleging that you cannot make the hair white or black." In this interpretation Jesus' injunctions are left without supporting reasons. Modern attempts to mitigate the passage on oaths, or at least to exempt oaths required by civil authority, receive no support from the rhetoric of the passage as a whole. As in the case of adultery or divorce, Jesus' commandments are absolutes, allowing no exceptions. This radical consistency greatly contributes to their arresting power.

In the final heading, on the extension of love of neighbor to include love of enemies, logical arguments are certainly introduced, and there are also other changes making the passage more argumentative, the chief of which are the rhetorical questions. There have been no rhetorical questions earlier in the headings and only one earlier in the sermon, occurring in the proem (5:13). Rhetorical question is primarily a device of audience contact, probably needed at this point in the speech after the exceedingly austere tone which has now been maintained since verse 17. Matthew thus shows Jesus as engaging himself directly with the audience in a passage which provides a transition between the style of the first group of headings and the second. It is here also that Jesus contrasts his audience with tax collectors and gentiles, another form of audience contact.

The second part of the proof (6:1–18) continues the series of commandments, but no longer in the form of an extended interpretation of scriptural authority. Instead, Jesus gives the injunctions on his own authority, amplifying and illustrating his meaning. The result is often to create enthymemes, the acceptance of which is encouraged by realistic detail familiar to his audience, by comparison, and by analogy. It is possible that this change in style reflects a change in Matthew's source, but his retention of the style of his source would derive, as argued above, from a feeling that it is somehow right.

At 6:1 Jesus is made to restate the thesis of 5:20 as an enthymeme. The major premise, which is assumed, would be "You should beware what the Father will not reward." The minor premise: "The Father will not reward *dikaiosyne* practiced before men." Conclusion: "Beware of practicing your *dikaiosyne* before men." The enthymeme is given some amplification in the phrases "in order to be seen by them," which explains "before men," and "by your Father who is in heaven." These amplifications are set at the ends of the clauses and linked by homoeoteleuton: both end in *ois* in Greek. Verses 2–4 apply the general commandment to almsgiving as a form of *dikaiosyne*, 5–15 to prayer, 16–18 to fasting. The units are cast in parallel forms, each of which involves an antithesis: "When you do this, do not . . . ; but when you do this, do . . . ." The negative half of the antithesis in each case is characterized as the action of the hypocrites, and the assertion inserted, "Truly,

I say to you, they have received their reward." The effect of this sentence in each case is to reintroduce the minor premise of the enthymeme of 6:1, which governs the entire passage. In 6:2 the second person singular suddenly appears, particularizing the situation as if Jesus pointed to some one person in the audience. The picture of the hypocrites is amplified in 6:2 and 6:5 by the doublet "in the synagogues and in the streets," and the action of the just man in 6:6 by detailing the stages of his action: go into your room, shut the door, pray. In late Greek rhetoricians the latter technique is known as *ap' arches achri telous*, "from beginning to end." The effect of this, as of the doubling, is to create *enargeia*, a vivid picture of the action. The same is true of the phrase "anoint your head and wash your face." The metaphors "sound no trumpet" and "do not let your left hand know what your right hand is doing" also contribute to the vividness of the passage, and that vividness in turn helps to make clear what Jesus means and contributes to his persuasiveness. Tropes and figures are thus used for persuasive effect.

The parallelism of the passage 6:1–18 is broken by the insertion of 6:7–15 (the Lord's Prayer), but without disturbing its symmetry, since the result is the elaboration of the second, or middle, of the three examples. The prayer is the centerpiece of the sermon, occurring just past its midpoint, a location favored by Demosthenes for the emotional climax in his greatest speeches. If, as is possible, Matthew has drawn the prayer from a different source, he has inserted it artfully. The passage stands out also in that the foil here is not the hypocrites, as in the surrounding passages, but the gentiles, with their repetitive prayers to many-named pagan gods. Rhetorically speaking, the first clause of the Lord's Prayer links it with the thesis of 6:1. The prayer itself is divided into two main parts: 6:9–10, which focus on God, and 6:11–13, which focus on "us." The prayer is, however, complex in structure, with parts interlocking in various ways; for example, the three initial imperatives with the homoeoteluton of *sou* ("your") in verses 9–10 form a unity, but the two *hos* ("as") clauses link verses 10 and 12. Extensive analysis of its rhythms is of debatable value, since we do not know exactly how the words were pronounced, but the concluding rhythms (*clausulae*) of each colon do in fact conform to those approved in the rhetorical schools: three cretics (- ˇ -), a fourth paean (ˇ ˇ ˇ -), a choriamb (- ˇ ˇ -), and four spondees (- -), of which one is preceded by a cretic (- ˇ -) and the last is a part of a dichoree (- ˇ - ˇ). The rhythms of the concluding verse (6:13) are especially weighty because of the preponderance of long syllables. Verses 14 and 15 are appended to the prayer, and when taken together with verse 12, constitute a hypothetical enthymeme; but within the prayer itself the only logical devices are the similes of verses 10 and 12, which imply the reasonableness of the immediately preceding clause. Unfortunately, the rhetorical qualities of the prayer do not seem to provide a basis for interpreting its obscurities, such as the meaning of "daily bread" (a literal translation would be "bread for the coming day"). "Bread" is certainly a metaphor, the only one in the prayer, but whether a weak metaphor for "sustenance" or a bold metaphor for the coming of the kingdom cannot easily be said.

From 6:19 to 7:20 follows a third group of headings, not anticipated quite as specifically as the others in the proposition of 5:17–20, but still inherent in the injunction of 5:20 that the audience's righteousness must exceed that of scribes and Pharisees. Several can be said to fall under the general class of forms of *dikaiosyne* (for example, "Judge not that you be not judged"), and all continue the theme of extending the meaning of commandments into a radical ethic, which will be summarized in the epilogue. These commandments in the third group are enunciated with authority, but supported by logos, or rational argument. Many of them take the form of enthymemes, and the basis of acceptance of the premises is largely common human experience or observance: knowledge of the ways of thieves, of the conditions of service, of the birds of the air or the grass of the field, or the speck in the eye, or of fish and serpents, or of good trees and bad. An analogy is thus established between the world of nature and the life of the farmer, on the one hand, and righteousness and the will of the Father on the other. Verses 6:19–21 may be taken as an example. The *hopou*, or "where," clause provides the reason why one should not lay up treasure on earth and should lay it up in heaven. The doublets "moth and rust" and "break in and steal" amplify and help to make the passage vivid. Verse 21, "For where your treasure is, there will your heart be also," draws a general conclusion from the two preceding enthymemes. The term *epicheireme* was used by some rhetoricians to describe such an argument in which a conclusion is drawn from two enthymemes, or from two statements, each with its justification. Verses 22–23 constitute an enthymeme of almost syllogistic validity. The major premise is the striking metaphorical definition "The eye is the lamp of the body." Then follows the hypothetical minor premise, "If your eye is sound, your whole body will be full of light," leading to the conclusion, which is stated as a figure of thought: "If then the light in you is darkness, how great the darkness!" The effect of the exclamation, really a rhetorical question, is to increase audience contact by confrontation. The rhetoric of Jesus as presented by Matthew is highly confrontational.

After another enthymeme in 6:24, a comparatively long passage, verses 25–34, supports the injunction not to be anxious about life. The evidence is a comparison to nature, with most of the examples stated as rhetorical questions. Inserted in it as amplification is a vivid scene in which troubled men are dramatically imagined asking "What shall we eat? or What shall we drink? or What shall we wear?" These are rejected as questions characteristic of the foil group, the gentiles. In verse 34 Jesus summarizes what he has said with a vigorous personification: "Tomorrow will be anxious for itself," to which is added a *gnome*, or *sententia*, a piece of general folk wisdom: "Let the day's own trouble be sufficient for the day." Throughout the sermon there is repetition of related words, which creates a gnomic effect. Treasuring up treasure in heaven is an example in the Greek of 6:19.

An even more striking example is found in the enthymeme

of the first two verses of chapter 7: "Judge not that you be not judged. For with the judgment you pronounce you will be judged, and the measure you give will be the measure you get." The *paronomasia*, or word play, is more extreme in the Greek text than in translation. Verses 7:3 and 7:4 are both stated as rhetorical questions and, like 6:2, employ the second person singular rather than the plural which has been maintained through most of the speech. It is again as though Jesus were singling out individuals in his audience. This strident tone, which could be said to constitute pathos, reaches its climax in the vocative, "You hypocrite," of verse 5. This completes the heading on judgment which began in 7:1.

Verse 7:6 is a very short heading on the treatment of things holy, which suffers in comparison to what precedes and what follows because of its lack of amplification. It is, however, an excellent example of chiasmus. The order of the subjects is reversed in the second half so that the reader must understand swine as the subject of "trample them under foot" and "dogs" as the subject of "turn to attack you." Note that we have returned to "you" in the plural.

The heading "Ask, and it will be given you" is given amplification analogous to that of "Judge not, that you be not judged," including rhetorical questions. The whole constitutes an epicheireme with enthymematic parts. The hypothetical minor premise of verse 11 makes use of the topic of the more and the less: "If you then, who are evil, know how to give good gifts to your children, how much more will your father in heaven give good things to those who ask him!" The Golden Rule functions as the conclusion in verse 12, given in positive form here, rather than in the negative form seen elsewhere, to emphasize positive action. It is noteworthy that Jesus feels impelled to strengthen it with an appeal to external authority: "for this is the law and the prophets."

The final two headings of the speech are the injunction to enter by the narrow gate (7:13–14) and the warning against false prophets (7:15–20). Both have a threatening tone of pathos. The first is treated briefly, much as the injunction on holiness of verse 6; the second is amplified like 7:1–5 and 7:7–12. The overall treatment of the headings of the third group, beginning at 6:19, is thus unamplified (6:19–21), unamplified (6:22–23), unamplified (6:24), much amplified (6:25–34), amplified (7:1–5), unamplified (7:6), amplified (7:7–12), unamplified (7:13–14), amplified (7:15–20). In each case the amplification involves the use of one or more rhetorical questions and of an analogy with nature or with everyday life easily understandable to Jesus' audience. The amplified headings do not seem to be the more important ones; thus it is in this part of the speech that one is most inclined to suspect a combination of materials originally delivered on different occasions, or selective elaboration on the part of the evangelist. The tone throughout the section is unmitigating, especially in contrast to the gentler tone of the sections containing the Beatitudes and the Lord's Prayer. Few orators could have delivered the sermon successfully, but the warnings of the Hebrew prophets did constitute some precedent for Jesus, and his teaching therefore did not fall into a genre with which his audience was entirely unfamiliar. It is a pity that Matthew tells us nothing about Jesus' delivery except for noting that he sat. He clearly believed it was Jesus' intention to alarm his audience, though the contents could be delivered in a calm and gentle manner to win their hearts as well.

Verses 7:21–27 are the epilogue of the sermon. According to most rhetoricians, an epilogue has two functions: it recapitulates the major point or points of the speech, and it seeks to stir the audience to action. Here, verses 21–23 perform the first function, 24–27 the second. Predictably, there is no argumentation, no enthymeme. Jesus summarizes his teaching with the words "Not every one who says to me, 'Lord, Lord,' shall enter the kingdom of heaven, but he who does the will of my Father who is in heaven." It is interesting that the focus of attention is dramatically turned to Jesus himself, who has played little part in the speech save for the "I" passages in the first section of headings. This completes the speech by involving the entire cast of characters: the Father in Heaven, Jesus the teacher, and the audience before him, referred to first in the third person, then in the second plural. There is an ominous sound in the plural of "I never knew you [*humas*]." Most will be lost. We have come a long way from the reassurances which gained audience goodwill in the proem.

The tone is somewhat mitigated by the final appeal, the similes of the wise and foolish to the builders of houses on rock or on sand; but even here it must be noted that the dire simile is put last, and it is with the fall of the house that Jesus leaves his audience. The two similes are each given some amplification in a parallel way and could be said to constitute ecphrases, or picturesque descriptions. Classical orators do not use ecphrases at the end of a speech, but Greek and Latin poets sometimes do.

Is the Sermon on the Mount good rhetoric? It has unity of thought. Within this unity it has a diversity of tone which gives it a sense of movement, from the gentleness and hope of the Beatitudes to the rigor of Jesus' interpretation of the law, softened somewhat in the Lord's Prayer, to the unmitigating severity of the concluding section. This is the sequence in which it must be heard. Audience contact is maintained throughout. Jesus or Matthew may indeed be said to play upon the feelings of the audience. The authoritative ethos is awesome, but it repeatedly utilizes the form of logical argument with premises based on nature and experiences well known to the audience. The rhetorical devices—tropes, figures, topics—are not ornaments, but functional within the thought, creating audience contact and intensity. Matthew says that the original audience was astounded at the speech. It has continued to startle and challenge readers for two thousand years.

In the sixth chapter of Luke, Jesus is described as coming down with his disciples from a mountain onto a level place and there addressing a large multitude. The sermon he delivers

(6:20–49) is a counterpart to the Sermon on the Mount in Matthew and overlaps significantly with it both in teaching and in illustrative material, but the situation Luke describes and the rhetorical qualities of the sermon he reports also differ significantly from what we find in Matthew. Some of the differences may be attributed to Luke himself. For example, writing for a largely gentile audience, he may have omitted references to the Jewish law found in his sources, on the ground that they would not be meaningful; it was also clearly expedient to avoid reference to the gentiles as a foil group, a device employed effectively in the sermon in Matthew. But even so, enough differences remain to suggest that Luke may have had in mind a different occasion.

The rhetorical unit in Luke has a clear beginning (6:20) and a clear ending (7:1), but its integrity is disturbed by the intrusion of Luke's voice in 6:39: "He also told them a parable." This is consistent with Luke's historiographic style, but it also suggests that Jesus said more than Luke reports. Some of the headings found in Matthew, but not in Luke, presumably are among the things omitted; there is throughout less amplification and less argumentation. Luke's sermon is a literary version, too concise to be orally effective with a large crowd and leaving too many things unexplained. Some of these things are given explanation elsewhere in Luke and could be consulted by a reader, but they would not have been clear to an audience that heard only what is reported here.

Who is this audience? In 6:13 Jesus is with a group described as "disciples," from among whom he chooses twelve who are named "apostles," an event not specifically mentioned by Matthew. He comes down from the mountain with the apostles and stands on a level place with "a great crowd of disciples"—the disciples in the larger sense of the word as we meet them later in Acts 1:15—"and a great multitude of people from all Judea and Jerusalem and the seacoast of Tyre and Sidon, who came to hear him and to be healed of their diseases" (6:17). The distinction between the crowd of disciples and the multitude of people suggests a greater diversity and less initial sympathy than is found in the rhetorical situation as described by Matthew. In Luke's Gospel Jesus has already met with the hostility of the Pharisees (6:2, 7), which is not true of the rhetorical context given by Matthew to the Sermon on the Mount, and Luke's sermon contains a passage which seems to indicate the presence of hostile individuals in the audience. Jesus begins his speech immediately with an address in the second person plural; though at first it might thus be assumed that he regards the larger group of disciples as constituting the audience, when the blessed of verses 20–23 are balanced against the cursed of 24–26, it becomes clear that Jesus is addressing the entire assembled group, both those sympathetic to him and those hostile.

In Matthew the exigence for speech is attributable solely to Jesus. In Luke the crowd has come not only to be healed, but "to hear him" (6:17), and the crowd is somewhat pushy, anxious "to touch him" (6:19). Another difference in the rhetorical situation is that Luke does not say that Jesus sat. He is clearly standing in 6:17, and then goes through the crowd healing, and finally speaks. Possibly we should imagine the crowd seated on the ground and Jesus standing in order to be seen. This makes Jesus into more of the figure of an orator as understood in the classical world. A final difference in the rhetorical situation is that Luke does not comment on the effect of the sermon on the audience. Yet elsewhere in his Gospel he shows interest in such matters (for example, 4:22, 32, 36; 5:26). It is tempting to try to read something into this. Is Luke implying that the sermon was not very effective?

The structure of the speech is much less clear in Luke than in Matthew. Luke gives us a proem (6:20–26) and follows this abruptly in 6:27 with the word "But." Its significance here is not clear, but it probably masks omission of reference to the law and compression of material. Perhaps 6:27–31 should be regarded as a proposition, but there is no specific distribution of the headings into groups. Luke has the substance of Matthew's epilogue, but he has converted the recapitulation into a rather querulous rhetorical question (6:46). Instead of the

internal dynamics of Matthew's speech, with its gentler passages, tightened into an ominous conclusion, Luke's maintains
a persistent polarization starting in the proem and continuing
throughout the epilogue: some are blessed and some cursed,
some will hearken and some not, some build on a rock and
some without a foundation. Why this should be, there is no
explanation.

Matthew's rhetorical consciousness is seen in the clear deliberative focus of his speech. Luke's speech too must be classified as deliberative, but this is less clearly brought out. Only
verses 27–38 really contain advice for the future. The rest is
predominantly praise and blame, that is to say, epideictic, and
nowhere does the sermon present the great promise of the
kingdom of God as an incentive to action.

Luke's proem is antithetical: four beatitudes, with amplification of the fourth in the climactic position, balanced against
the four coordinated curses. As in Matthew, the paradoxical
nature of the first beatitude attracts attention, but it really does
not embrace a wide variety of sympathy in its appeal. To some
extent this is mitigated by the organization: the poor are mentioned first, and those that hunger and those that weep may be
regarded as subdivisions of them. A parallel structure describes
the rich, who are now full and happy. But no attempt is made
to urge the rich to give to the poor and to attain the kingdom;
they are simply cursed and rejected.

The commandments of 6:27–31 are a single compressed list.
None takes the form of an enthymeme, but that is not surprising if we regard them collectively as a proposition. In 32–36 the
commandments are taken up, and support is given by the dialectical principle of the rule of contradictories: Jesus posits the
opposite premise and then introduces an example to refute it.
Some liveliness is imparted to the passage by the use of rhetorical questions. The commandments of 37–38 are given some
logical support by being reciprocal and could be restated as
enthymemes, but the paratactic style reduces the logical impact. Verse 38 has an interesting rhetorical feature: "Give, and
it will be given to you; good measure, pressed down, shaken

together, running over, will be put into your lap." These are a series of steps "from beginning to end," emphasized by *asyndeton*, or omission of connexions. The climax is more obvious in the Greek than in the English. What are described as parables begin in verse 39. They are in fact only a series of analogies which might be developed into Jesus' characteristic parables but are not so treated here, and those in verses 39–40 are somewhat obscure. In verse 41, as in Matthew 7:3, we have suddenly the second person singular, leading to the apostrophe "O hypocrite!" Verses 43–45 resemble Matthew 7:15–20, but with the omission of any reference to false prophets, which gives point to Matthew's passage, and the premises are not so logically arranged. The result is to mitigate the effectiveness of the whole. Verse 46 is an obscured recapitulation. Matthew's concluding picture of the two houses is superior to that of Luke in the specificity of the house "built on sand," which in Luke is merely built on the earth without foundation.

Luke 6 is not a very good speech. What persuasive power Luke's speech has inheres almost solely in the ethos, or authority, of Jesus. In Matthew too ethos is primary, but more attempt is made to couch statements in logical form, and greater pathos is achieved.

Behind the rhetoric of the two evangelists in these sermons stands their perception of the rhetoric of Jesus, and behind that perception stands the actual rhetoric of Jesus. The last of these, first in chronological sequence, cannot be objectively determined, but it may be possible to make some suggestions about the evangelists' perception or preconceptions of the rhetoric of Jesus. They sought to give a picture of Jesus in which they believed and in which they wished others to believe.

It seems possible that Jesus delivered something like the Sermon on the Mount and the Sermon on the Plain and even more likely that the evangelists thought he did so, however they may have gone about trying to construct the text of such a sermon. Jesus was a teacher who conveyed his message orally to a variety of audiences. Most speakers who present a cause to different audiences at different places, as Jesus did preaching in Palestine, develop a basic speech which encapsulates their main views in a way that proves effective. When presenting the speech to different audiences, the speaker may elaborate or shorten it as conditions seem to require, sometimes inserting topical references, sometimes borrowing portions of the speech to use in other contexts. This is a common practice among modern political candidates (reporters get used to hearing essentially the same speech at each stop), and it is true of modern evangelists as well. So viewed, the occurrence of two versions of Jesus' teaching, one set on a hill and one on a plain, is not surprising. Luke may simply have preserved a shorter version of what he regarded as Jesus' characteristic preaching early in his ministry. Nor is it surprising that other Gospels contain in other contexts phrases reminiscent of the sermon in Matthew. Jesus was engaged in oral teaching, and he frequently repeated himself.

The authenticity of Matthew's version has been questioned on the ground that no one could have remembered a specific sermon in such detail and that therefore Matthew made it up from a written collection of Jesus' sayings. But if a speech was repeatedly delivered in slightly different versions in the presence of the disciples, given their devotion to Jesus and the striking nature of what he said, few of them would have had difficulty in dictating a version at some later time for readers who had not personally heard Jesus. Matthew's version might thus represent what was remembered from several occasions and not what Jesus said verbatim at any one delivery; but in the same sense it could represent a relatively full version of what he was remembered as saying at one period of his ministry. Quotations from such a "speech" could then have been utilized in different contexts and even have been recollected into an anthology of "sayings." In a recent article (see Bibliography) Hans Dieter Betz has suggested that Matthew's source could have been an "epitome" of Jesus' teaching, analogous to the epitome of classical philosophers.

The Gospels each present an account of Jesus' life and teaching in a narrative sequence. It is possible that these sequences are not historical and result from an attempt to order information about Jesus into a probable sequence of events; the account by Mark perhaps establishes the basic outline. In the two sermons in Matthew and Luke which we have been considering, Jesus gives a comparatively systematic account of his teaching and is presented as doing so at an early point in his career, soon after gathering his disciples, though addressing a wider crowd. In Mark also he preaches in synagogues (1:21) and in other settings (2:2, 2:13), but no extended discourse is attributed to him. Preaching in synagogues is likely to have taken its form from exegesis of scriptural readings—what is referred to in Matthew as "you have heard it said, . . . but I say to you." In chapters 2 and 3 of Mark, Jesus is shown using parables to answer questions, and finally (4:2) he addresses a large crowd, teaching them "many things in parables."

It is possible that these accounts reflect a belief on the part of the evangelists in a real or probable change in Jesus' rhetorical strategy. Audience reaction to the Sermon on the Mount is said by Matthew (7:28) to be one of astonishment. Jesus' authority was perceived (7:29), but the word "astonished" (*exeplessonto*) also suggests some inability to comprehend the meaning of what Jesus said. Luke, uncharacteristically, says nothing about the effect of the Sermon on the Plain, and this may mask a similar belief in some failure of the crowd to understand Jesus' message. The Pharisees, when they encounter Jesus (in all three synoptic Gospels), clearly do experience some intellectual reaction to what he says, primarily a negative response to what they perceive as an inconsistency between the content of his teaching and the Jewish law. The evidence of Matthew 13, Mark 4, and Luke 8 seems to suggest a perceived crisis in Jesus' rhetoric, a decision to abandon attempts to explain his message to a popular audience in a partially deductive form and to rely instead on inductive argument with an unstated conclusion as seen in the parables. The parables were popular, and they had the advantage of being less provoking to the Pharisees or other groups because they avoided the enunciation of commandments in conflict with the law. A result of this change in rhetoric, however, would have been the abandonment of any attempt to impart understanding of Jesus' message to some kinds of hearers: the more worldly, sophisticated, and probably better educated, for whom an explicit conclusion and some use of deductive argument was meaningful. Jesus apparently (as perceived by the evangelists) concluded that he could not reach them. Let us look briefly at the account of this in each gospel.

In Matthew 12 Jesus has some unpleasant encounters with Pharisees. He tries to avoid them and after one session of healing asks those present not to talk about what he has done (12:16). Later in the same day, however, he again addresses a crowd, limiting his remarks to parables (13:3), with the concluding injunction "He who has ears, let him hear." The disciples are surprised at this: "Why do you speak to them in parables?" (13:10). If that had been his consistent style, it is unlikely that they would have asked. His reply is to draw a sharp distinction between the disciples, to whom it has been given to know the secrets of the kingdom of heaven, and others, who do not hear and do not understand (13:11–13). He explains his decision by quoting from Isaiah 6:9–10. In its original context that passage is apparently intended to provoke the people to react, to dissociate themselves from those who will not hear Isaiah's message, and it is given powerful ethos by being attributed directly to God. But in Matthew, addressed only to the disciples, the quotation does not have that effect. It simply rejects many as unable to understand and refuses to hold out to them any opportunity to change.

Much of Matthew's account is identical with that in Mark, but instead of reporting the scriptural quotation, Mark has Jesus say on his own authority that he speaks in parables, "lest they should turn again, and be forgiven" (Mark 4:12). Matthew may be thought to have tried to construct a more probable scene in which Jesus, confronted with the failure of his efforts at teaching, has turned to the prophet for an explanation of it. As we have seen, Mark was aware of previous efforts at preaching by Jesus, but for his account they are of little importance. Some were chosen, others not. That can mean that the preaching was unsuccessful.

Now it might be objected to this that the Sermon on the Mount already reveals a very fatalistic attitude toward certain groups, but there is an important difference. The rejection of scribes, tax collectors, Pharisees, and gentiles in the sermon as predestined to damnation is a public rejection of groups which contains within it the possibility of inciting any individual in the audience to cast his lot with the saved. The rejection of the groups can be viewed as a rhetorical device to save the individual. Beginning in Matthew 13 and Mark 4 this is no longer true, and Jesus communicates his acceptance of the fact to the disciples.

The account in Luke is slightly muted. Instead of asking Jesus why he has suddenly begun teaching in parables, the disciples ask Jesus to explain a specific parable, that of the sower (8:9), and neither the quotation from Isaiah nor the crucial phrase in the summary of Mark, "lest they should turn again and be forgiven," is included. Here, as often, Luke is engaged in editorial work, better fitting his text for a wider readership.

Parables could have been useful to Jesus in avoiding confrontation with the Pharisees, but they would have been equally useful in maintaining communication with that part of the wider public who represented Jesus' main hope of a sympathetic audience, those attracted by his ability as a healer and those not committed to a worldly life. He never explains this to the disciples and perhaps could not do so because it would involve terms in which neither he nor they thought. It is unlikely that Jesus conceptualized his own rhetoric. The parables function like myths in a traditional, unphilosophical society. A myth does not have to be explained and can be directly apprehended without conceptualization. Its truth can be felt and the truth applied to a mythical understanding of the world around one. The more sophisticated, the more given to conceptualization, the more trained in legal formulae the audience, the more difficult it becomes for them to apprehend myth directly. Jesus as portrayed in the synoptic Gospels apparently comes to feel that the audience he can reach does not need self-conscious, structured thought. Within that audience, there remains some hope of converts. Thus he does not abandon all efforts at preaching, but speaks in terms that only some can understand. He is particularly delighted when he encounters someone who is mythopoeic, as is illustrated by his exchange with the Canaanite woman described in Matthew 15:21–28 and Mark 7:24–30.

After arrival in Jerusalem, toward the end of his ministry, Jesus is in a much more complex rhetorical setting, and occasionally then he is shown as reverting to a more logical exposition of his teaching. The invective against the Pharisees in Matthew 23 (a fine example of the epideictic species of rhetoric) is prefaced (23:2–12) by a rational explanation of why he finds them so offensive. This is addressed to a crowd and also to the disciples and any Pharisees within hearing, and its logical qualities are to be explained by the mix of people to be found in that urban audience, where even Jesus' supporters can be expected to be more educated, more sophisticated.

There thus seems some justification for the belief that the writers of the synoptic Gospels, and Matthew in particular, perceived a crisis in the rhetoric of Jesus. Whether that crisis was historically authentic, or whether it represents a later perception of what might have happened, given the evidence the evangelists had and their own rhetorical sensitivity, I do not know.

Chapter Three. Epideictic Rhetoric:
John 13–17

Epideictic is the most difficult to define of the three universal species of rhetoric. It is commonly regarded as the oratory of praise or blame. Aristotle sought (*Rhetoric* 1.3.1358a) to make a basic distinction between situations in which the audience are judges and those in which they are only spectators or observers. In a sense, epideictic is thus everything that does not fall clearly into the category of judicial or deliberative, everything that does not clearly focus on the judgment of a past action, either defending it or attacking it, or on the expediency or inexpediency of a specific future action by the audience. Epideictic as Aristotle knew it consisted of public funeral orations delivered in Greek cities, such as that ascribed to Pericles in the second book of Thucydides' *History of the Peloponnesian War*; or panegyrics, speeches given at festivals and celebrating the occasion or the city or the divine and human founders of the festivals; or the display pieces of sophists, such as Gorgias' *Encomium of Helen*, which primarily illustrate the art of the sophist in invention and style. As Aristotle subsequently admits (2.18.1391b), the audience in such cases becomes a judge, but a judge of the eloquence of the speaker rather than of his cause. Yet funeral orations and panegyrics were intended to be persuasive and often imply some need for actions, though in a more general way than does deliberative oratory. Greek orators regularly sought to give significance to their words by holding up the past as worthy of imitation in the future, and in the Roman empire epideictic orations celebrating the virtues of a ruler, Pliny's panegyric of Trajan for example, often came to praise

not the virtues he actually had, but virtues the orator thought
he should cultivate. They thus take on a more or less subtle
deliberative purpose.

Some rhetoricians anxious to increase the grip of their discipline upon society came to classify all of literature, including
epic and dramatic poetry, as subdivisions of epideictic. Modern rhetoricians stress the situational or occasional exigence
which produces epideictic, the need provided by conventional
etiquette or the speaker's personal feelings to honor someone
or observe some holiday—commencement or the Fourth of
July would be good examples. They also emphasize as the chief
goal of epideictic the strengthening of audience adherence to
some value, as the basis for a general policy of action. In this
sense most modern preaching is epideictic, for it usually aims
to strengthen Christian belief and induce a congregation to
lead the Christian life. Only when a preacher has some very
definite action in mind does the sermon become deliberative—
if he is seeking to persuade a group to receive baptism or to
give up drinking, for example. Occasionally a sermon may also
be judicial, as when a preacher seeks to answer objections
raised against the authority or teaching of Christ or against his
own actions. But in true judicial situations the audience must
have the authority to implement a judgment, as a synod does.
When a preacher inveighs against some group for irreligious
or immoral actions and his congregation has no power to act
against them, he is practicing invective, the negative form of
epideictic. A New Testament example is Jesus' invective against
the Pharisees in Matthew 23.

Epideictic passages regularly occur in other species of oratory and are especially common in proems or epilogues where
the need arises to secure a favorable hearing or move an addressee to take some action. Although classical rhetoricians
and most of their successors have taught that epideictic is a
distinct species of rhetoric, it is also possible to speak of an
epideictic style or color added to discourse of any species. Judicial or deliberative speech may display this color to the extent that attention is given to belief or attitude, and all dis-

course not calling for specific action displays it in varying degrees. In a lecture on mathematics it is slight, for the speaker restricts himself to logos and is content if the audience understands his proofs; in a lecture on the humanities it is greater, in that the speaker probably wishes the audience to share some of his values. The epideictic style tends to amplification and is fond of ornament and tolerant of description and digression. Its virtue is imagination and inspiration; its characteristic vices are factual inaccuracy—epideictic orators are notoriously casual about their use of history—and tolerance of flattery, for the epideictic orator usually wants to be admired, whereas the judicial or deliberative orator may be content with a majority of one in the final vote.

The connexion of epideictic with occasions begets a variety of conventional forms differing in different societies. The original Greek forms were the funeral oration or *epitaphios logos*, the festival panegyric, and the sophistic exercise, sometimes called *paignion* or plaything. With the collapse of the Greek democracies and their replacement by centralized, often autocratic, government, addresses to kings, governors, and other powerful people became more important. Public epideictic in the Roman empire was mirrored in private life by speeches at birthdays and weddings and on the arrival or departure of friends and relatives. Although rhetorical handbooks such as those of Aristotle, Cicero, and Quintilian regularly give some general account of epideictic, they do not describe these separate forms. Students learned how to speak on such occasions partly from the exercises they had practiced in grammar schools, partly from imitation of speeches they had read or had heard. The grammar-school exercises included the composition of encomia in praise of a person, place, or thing. A student was expected to make a systematic utilization of suggested topics: of a person, for example, his city, ancestors, parents, education, career, and his moral virtues.

In later antiquity a few handbooks of epideictic were compiled, of which the most important are two treatises attributed to Menander Rhetor, composed perhaps around A.D. 300. An excellent edition, with English translation, has recently been published by D. A. Russell and N. G. Wilson. Menander's handbooks describe the many different forms of epideictic and what were regarded as their appropriate topics. Two of the forms are more personal than the others and can indeed involve a deliberate abandonment of conventional structure and topics: the *lalia* and the *monody*. A lalia is an informal talk and could be practiced even on quite grand occasions. Sometimes professional sophists, as teachers of rhetoric are called in later antiquity, liked to illustrate their versatility by giving both a speech in the traditional form—say a prosphonetic, or address to an arriving dignitary—and a lalia, or personal reaction to the occasion. Epideictic passages of a personal nature in the Bible, including John 13–17, could be termed laliae. A monody is an emotional lament, not entirely unlike some passages in the prophets, usually on the death of a person or the destruction of a city. The most famous is Aelius Aristides' monody on the destruction of Smyrna by an earthquake in A.D. 178.

Two of the forms discussed by Menander are the *propemptic* (2.5), a speech for one departing, of which Luke 10 provides a biblical example, and the *syntactic* (2.15), or speech of leave-taking. The latter is another possible label for John 13–17, as well as for Paul's farewell speech to the elders of Ephesus in Acts 20, though neither accord with the topics listed by Menander. Christians, however, did eventually adopt classical topics. An early example is the speech of farewell addressed to Origen by Gregory Thaumaturgos in A.D. 238, and in the fourth century there emerges an almost complete synthesis of Christian and classical epideictic forms. The finest example, and one of the greatest speeches of all time, is Gregory of Nazianzus' funeral oration for Basil the Great, delivered around A.D. 381.

Menander also (2.9) lists the *paramythetic*, or consolation, as an epideictic form. As oratory, it is usually incorporated into a funeral oration, but consolations in the form of an epistle are also common. Paramythetic is probably the best classical term to describe Jesus' consolation of the disciples in John 13–17.

Consolatory speeches by one about to die can be found in classical literature, for example at the end of Plato's *Apology* and *Phaedo* and in Tacitus' account of the death of Seneca (*Annals* 15.62). Deathbed speeches attributed to great figures of the Old Testament are a traditional Jewish form, but consolation is not their function (see especially Genesis 49, Deuteronomy 31, 1 Samuel 12, 1 Chronicles 28). Some of Jesus' words, however, have counterparts in the topics of a traditional classical consolation. Menander suggests, for example, that one should say that the deceased has enjoyed enough of life, that he has escaped its pains, that he is now living with gods, and a speaker can even find fault with those who lament the deceased. He should be blessed as a god and placated as superhuman.

There are a number of passages in the New Testament which seem primarily epideictic: the Magnificat (Luke 1:46–55) is clearly one. Philippians is largely epideictic, as is 2 Peter and Jesus' invective against the Pharisees in Matthew 23, though that is part of a longer judicial unit. Whether or not a classical rhetorician would regard John 13–17 as a consolation, it is clearly epideictic, for Jesus is concerned with the disciples' attitudes, feelings, and beliefs at his departure from life in this world, and though he gives a new commandment to them and talks about the difficulties they will face in the future, these issues are subsumed into their understanding of the present circumstances and reaction to them.

Redaction criticism stresses the similarity of themes in John 14 and 15–16 and points to the conclusion that the passages may be two separate versions of Jesus' farewell discourse. Rhetorical criticism, however, is interested in the text as we have it and how the editor and his early Christian audience may have perceived that entire text as a unit. Some speaker of Greek, at some time, arranged these chapters in what seemed to him an effective or appropriate sequence. Behind the rhetoric of this author or editor stands his perception of the rhetoric of Jesus. The rhetorical unit could be defined in several different ways. Chapter 14 is self-contained, as are chapters 15–16, but it may perhaps be interesting to give an example of how a rhetorical unit can be studied when it is defined as extending beyond the actual limits of a single speech. Together, chapters 13–17 appear to be built around amplification of a small number of topics which are enunciated in the beginning of 13.

The rhetorical situation of John 13–17 is clearly stated in 13. The occasion is the Last Supper. In the evangelist's account the exigence is supplied by the confusion and distress of the disciples and Jesus' concern that they should come to understand his mission. The questions or requests of Peter, Thomas, Philip, the other Judas, and the disciples as a group help to reveal Jesus' need to minister to them and to explain his coming departure. The audience is restricted to the disciples, a group made more cohesive by the common meal and also, as Jesus and the reader realize, by the departure of Judas Iscariot. The rhetorical problem, from the point of view of Jesus, is the distress of the disciples and their limited understanding of his nature and mission. From the point of view of the evangelist, the rhetorical problem is how to present the scene in such a way that both its pathos and its glory will emerge. The discourse is not found in the other Gospels, and all or part of it, especially chapter 17, may be a *prosopopoeia*, a rhetorical recreation of what Jesus might have said under these circumstances. Such forms were practiced in the rhetorical schools. We can imagine the evangelist seeking to reconstruct the scene and the discourse, not only from whatever oral tradition he had, but through prayerful meditation in search of inspiration. The reality and validity of inspiration were widely credited in the classical world, and inspiration was assumed to be a regular feature of poetic and sometimes of philosophic composition. The discipline provided by rhetoric helped to facilitate this process by providing structure and topics which the writer could work out and adapt to his needs.

Verse 13:1 constitutes a proem which immediately arrests the reader's attention. It is built on five material topics which will prove to be the basis of all that is to follow. Since we are engaged in rhetorical analysis, we call them "topics"; a literary

critic might prefer "themes," a theologian "doctrines," a philosopher "premises." They are ideas or facts which will be constantly restated in different words, in different order, and in
different form in what follows, and it may be convenient to
letter them for easy identification: "Now before the feast of the
Passover, (A) when Jesus knew (B) that his hour had come to
depart (C) out of this world to the Father, (D) having loved
(E) his own, he loved them to the end." Topic A is Jesus'
relation to the Father; B is Jesus' departure; C is the world; D
is love; E is Jesus' relation to the disciples. Topics A and E
develop a reciprocal relationship in the course of the passage.
Jesus' departure, we soon learn, implies a return and thus also
a reciprocal movement. Love is also reciprocal. The world is
antithetical to each of the other topics. The rhetorical unit as a
whole contains very little logical argument, but it maintains a
dynamic reciprocal relationship which functions as its logos,
reinforcing the major persuasive factor, Jesus' ethos, and rein-
forced by the pathos of the situation.

The proem is followed by a narration, as in a judicial speech.
Epideictic makes use of narrative when it needs it, but only
rarely requires a formal narration. Here, however, the evangelist has certain things he must tell us, important in themselves
and in later Christian doctrine, but also important in understanding the discourse which is to follow. The narration extends from 13:2 through 13:30. It fulfills the rhetorical require-
ment that a narration should be brief, rapid, and probable.
The technique is "from beginning to end," complete with dramatic dialogue, but we are not allowed to forget the topics of
the proem. Verse 3, "Jesus, knowing that the Father had given
all things into his hands, and that he had come from God and
was going to God," is built on topics A and B and becomes the
basis for Jesus' actions toward the disciples, topic E, in the next
verse. Topic E also dominates verses 12–20, which may be
viewed as amplification of it. At least one new topic emerges,
which will reappear, "the devil" in verse 2 (topic F). Jesus'
words in verse 7, "What I am doing you do not know now, but
afterwards you will understand," and in verse 19, "I tell you this

now, before it takes place, that when it does take place you may believe that I am he," are part of the logos; they call attention to what Aristotle would call a "sign," which will be confirmed and thus help to prove what he says. Verses 14–15 are an enthymeme, strengthened by the example given as a maxim in verse 16. Verse 18 utilizes evidence from Scripture, a common form of "external proof."

With the departure of Judas, described in 13:21–30, the narration ends. Verses 31–35 make up a remarkable rhetorical proposition. They restate the five topics of the proem of 13:1, and in exactly the same order: (A) Jesus' relationship to the Father, 31–32; (B and C) Jesus' departure from the world, 33; (D) the new commandment, "that you love one another," 34; and (E) Jesus' relationship to the disciples and theirs to him, "all men will know that you are my disciples," 35.

Then follows the interruption by Peter, the first of a series of interruptions into Jesus' discourse. These interruptions add a great deal of interest to the unit by their dramatic form and in the presentation of the ethos of the disciples and of Jesus' individual relationships to them. They also help to develop the basic topics of the proem and proposition in varied ways. The questions of Peter and Thomas relate to Jesus' departure, that of Philip to Jesus' relations to the Father, that of Judas to Jesus' relations to the world.

The main body of Jesus' consolation begins in 14:1: "Let not your hearts be troubled." As support for this injunction he offers a restatement of topic A: "You believe in God, believe also in me." The first half of the verse is a conclusion to be drawn from, or supported by, the second half. It is thus an enthymeme, but its premises are asserted and not proved. Their acceptability is thus dependent on Jesus' ethos. Verses 3–4 are also simple ethical assertions, but verse 2, "In my Father's house are many rooms; if it were not so would I have told you," employs a logical device, for Jesus uses the law of contradictories, stating the negative of the premise and refuting that with a sign as he does in the Sermon on the Plain (Luke 6:32–

36). Metaphors in this passage (14:1–4) lend reality to what is said: the Father's house, the rooms in it, the road to it.

The discourse is then interrupted, first by Thomas, then by Philip. In reply to Thomas' question, "How can we know the way?" Jesus replies by metaphor, "I am the way, and the truth, and the life," and by reasserting topic A, "No one comes to the Father, but by me," and then topic E, "If you had known me, you would have known my Father." If 14:7 is taken as a contrary-to-fact condition, it may reveal some irritation. Certainly some irritation is evident in the reply to Philip, where Jesus reasserts topic A not once, but three times: "He who has seen me has seen the Father" in verse 9; and "I am in the Father and the Father in me" and "the Father who dwells in me" in verse 10.

Verse 14:11 is wrongly paragraphed in the Revised Standard Version. The verb is in the second person plural, rather than in the singular Jesus has used with Philip, and introduces a new section. Jesus first reasserts topic A—for the fifth time in this part of the discourse—but supports it in a new way: "or else believe me for the sake of the works themselves." The section from verse 11 to verse 14 supports Jesus' assertion of consolation to the disciples by the evidence of works, both those he has done and those the disciples will be able to do. The evidence of works, usually miracles, and the evidence of Scripture are two foundations of external proof in Christian rhetoric, used primarily to support authority. In verse 12 there is the internal proof of argument in the form of the greater and the less. The section as a whole is built around two assertions of topic A and three assertions of topic E.

In verses 14:11–14 the evidence of works is a source of consolation; in a new section, 15–21, consolation is offered by the coming of the Holy Spirit (topic G). The nature of the Spirit is amplified, and thus emphasized, in verse 17, where it is set off against topic C, the world. Topics A and E repeatedly occur, and in verses 20–21 are linked together by topic D, love, first in ascending, then in descending, order: "He who has my commandments and keeps them, he it is who loves me; and he who loves me will be loved by my Father, and I will love him and manifest myself to him."

In the interruption at 14:22–24 Judas takes up topic C, the world, as it appears in the assertion of verse 17. Why will Jesus not manifest himself to the world? Jesus gives no immediate answer to this. His reply here is a simple assertion of topics A and D, first in the positive (verse 24), then in the negative (25). Some fuller answer is eventually offered at 15:18–27.

The discourse resumes in 14:25–30, which has elements of an epilogue. Jesus' presence with the disciples is mentioned first (topic E), then the Holy Spirit (topic G), then the Father "in my name" (topic A). The coming of the Spirit will bring re-membrance to the disciples, thus confirming Jesus' words. In a tricolon in verse 27 Jesus seems to give a benediction and re-peats and slightly amplifies the initial verse of the chapter, as though it were an *inclusio*. But verse 28 then repeats the topic of departure, reverses it into a promise of return, and then asserts the relationship of Jesus to the Father, topic A. All this, Jesus says (29), he has told "so that when it does take place, you may believe." In other words, its accomplishment, like the coming of the Spirit, is to be a "sign" of the truth of what he says. But the ruler of the world is coming (topics F and C). "He has no power over me; but I do as the Father has com-manded me, so that the world may know that I love the Father [topics A, C, D]. Rise, let us go hence."

This seems to mark a conclusion, but when chapter 15 opens Jesus is again speaking: "I am the true vine, and my Father is the vinedresser." The metaphor is given much amplification in a section which extends through verse 11, and it is referred to again in verse 16. The rhetorical function of the metaphor is to amplify topic E, the relationship of the disciples to Jesus, as is made clear in verses 3–4 and 7–8. In verse 9 this is then linked to topic A, Jesus' relation to the Father, and to topic D, love: "If you keep my commandments, you will abide in my love, just as I have kept my Father's commandments and abide in his love." The point of the whole is the consolation of the disciples as becomes clear in verse 11: "These things I have spoken to you, that my joy may be in you, and that your joy may be full."

The function of the next section, 15:12–17, is the amplification of topic D, love. In 15:12 the commandment of 13:34 is repeated and linked to topic B, Jesus' departure, in verse 13. Verses 13 and 14 together imply an enthymeme, with "friends" as the middle term, deriving from topic E. Verses 15–16 utilize a new image, the servant and the master, which is rejected for the new higher relationship of Jesus to the disciples (topic E) and its now regular linkage to topic A, the Father. Verse 17 repeats the commandment of love as a logical conclusion.

The section from 15:18 to 16:4 is an amplification of topic C, the world, set in opposition to love ("hate" in 15:18) and the relationship of Jesus to the disciples. The image of the servant and the master is taken up (verse 20) and applied to this opposed situation and some fuller explanation given of why Jesus cannot manifest himself to the world. Not only has the world rejected Jesus, but through this rejection it has sin in that it has rejected the Father, thus linking the antitheses of topics A and E. That this was to be expected is confirmed (verse 25) by the external evidence of the Psalms, the future witness of the Spirit, and the present witness of the disciples with their continuing relationship to Jesus (topic E). They must, however, expect a difficult time. Verses 16:1–4 make this explicit, but the fulfillment of Jesus' prophecy will itself constitute a sign of the truth of all that he has said.

At this point in the discourse all the original topics have been given amplification except for B, the matter of Jesus' departure. Jesus now turns to this (16:4b–28). He recognizes that it is the specific cause of the disciples' sorrow and thus of his need to console them (16:6). There is an inconsistency between his remark that none has asked where he is going and the question of Peter in 13:36, perhaps overlooked by the evangelist in assembling materials from his sources, though the question can be interpreted to mean that Jesus thinks the disciples are too concerned with the present moment and not enough with the kingdom of heaven. The first consolation he offers is the practical advantage to them (*sympherei humin*, 16:7) of the coming of the Spirit (topic G). This will become the solution to the problems created by the world as described in the previous section, for the Spirit will bring enlightenment and judgment to the world (8–11). The results of the Spirit's coming are amplified in 12–15, being united with topics A and E.

A second consolation Jesus offers is that though he will depart, he will come again (16:16). This occasions a dramatic interruption (verses 17–19) as the disciples express bewilderment among themselves. Jesus frankly acknowledges their distress at his departure (20), but likens it to a woman in travail and her joy at the birth of a child (21). So too, they will have full joy (22). With the reunion of Jesus and the disciples, topics A and B will perfectly merge into joy (23–24). Jesus says that he has been speaking in *paroimiai*, "by-words"; in classical Greek the term usually means "proverbs," not figured language, but it can be taken to mean "indirectly." This will no longer be necessary; all indirection and mediation will be swept away, and through love (topic D), Father, Son, and disciples will be united in direct communication (topics A, E; verse 27). This is what Jesus means by saying that he is leaving the world (topics B, C) and going to the Father (28).

Verses 16:29–33 are an epilogue to the section of the unit begun in 14:1, the consolation. The disciples express their intellectual and emotional release (29–30), and Jesus recapitulates his understanding of what will happen and his victory, which is the real source of consolation (33).

Chapter 17, Jesus' prayer to the Father, is a larger epilogue to the entire rhetorical unit. It is the actualization of the potential inherent in topic A, Jesus' claim of a unique relationship to the Father, and its objective is the actualization of the potential in topic E, the special relationship of the disciples to Jesus. It would thus seem to require the reader to assume that Jesus prays aloud, in the presence of the disciples, and that they hear what he says. Topic B, Jesus' departure, is mentioned (17:11, 13) and of course underlies the situation, but is not stressed. Topic

C, the world, is repeatedly mentioned beginning in verse 6, at first in the sense met earlier as the antithesis of the relationship of Jesus and the disciples, which reaches a climax in verse 16: "They are not of the world, even as I am not of the world." But beginning in verse 21, as the prayer nears its end, the world takes on a more neutral cast, as though it can still be won through belief and through Jesus' glory (esp. 23). At the end, however, Jesus returns to his relationship to the disciples (E) and the topic of love (D) which binds them and him and the Father. The prayer makes a splendid conclusion, recapitulating the topics presented earlier and providing an emotional fulfill- ment for the whole passage. Its persuasive qualities come al- most entirely from ethos and pathos, the latter not the distress of Jesus' death, but the joy of his transfiguration. Consolation is completed and celebration remains.

The most striking rhetorical feature of the unit as a whole is probably its repetitiveness. It is constructed almost entirely out of five basic topics, constantly restated, sometimes in the same, often in different words. The same ideas are remolded, their relationship to each other worked out, amplified, and eluci- dated, and a movement from one to the other posited. There is very little formal logical argument, though there is some use of external means of persuasion. But the topics themselves in the end function as the premises on which a kind of transcendent logic is constructed with the help of the authoritative ethos of Jesus. Although signs of editing of the sources remain (for example, 14:31 seems to link directly to 18:1; 16:5 seems incon- sistent with 13:36), the addition of chapters 15, 16, and 17 greatly deepens the understanding of the topics enunciated in chapters 13 and 14, and it was clearly these topics which were important to the evangelist. The construction of the unit is somewhat reminiscent of the dialogues in which Plato presents Socrates as engaged in a preliminary discussion of a subject which is then reopened in a deeper and more extensive way.

Chapter Four. Judicial Rhetoric:
Second Corinthians

S ince Jesus offers no defense before the Council and before Pilate, the principal judicial situations in the Gospels are his encounters with the Pharisees. In Matthew's Gospel there is an elaborate rhetorical unit stretching from 21:23 through the end of chapter 23 which can be viewed as judicial rhetoric and which consists of a preliminary altercation with the priests and elders, a series of parables relating to judgment, a renewed interrogation by the Pharisees, and an extended epilogue by Jesus denouncing them to the crowd (invective is a regular feature of judicial oratory). Matthew, however, was the primary subject of discussion in a previous chapter; it seems better to seek a different work for analysis here. Second Corinthians is the obvious choice, for it provides the most extended piece of judicial rhetoric in the New Testament. The judicial speeches in Acts can be left for consideration when we take up that book.

There has always been a close formal connexion between the oration and the epistle. The Greek "orator" Isocrates was too nervous to speak in public and wrote out his speeches for publication or to send to an addressee as an open letter. Some instruction in letter writing may occasionally have been given in grammar schools, and in later antiquity there were handbooks of letter writing which show the influence of rhetorical theory. The only Greek rhetorical treatise to give attention to the writing of letters is that by Demetrius, *On Style* (223–225), probably a work of the Hellenistic period. In the western Middle Ages instruction in letter writing became a major part of rhetoric, under the rubric *dictamen*. Although an epistle requires a salutation and a complimentary close, its body can take the form of a deliberative, epideictic, or judicial speech with the traditional parts and all the inventional and stylistic features of an oration. On delivery a letter was usually read aloud; thus audience perception of its contents followed the pattern of speech.

Paul's First Epistle to the Corinthians is largely deliberative, though it contains some judicial passages, for example 1:13–17 claiming that he had not created faction in Corinth and chapter 9 defending his rights as an apostle. Second Corinthians, on the other hand, is largely judicial except for chapters 8 and 9, which are deliberative. After a relatively simple salutation (1:1–2), Paul addresses the Corinthians in a proem (1:3–8) which is intended to reveal his goodwill toward them and secure their goodwill toward him. This is essential to his ethos. The topics on which he builds are the mercy of God, his own afflictions, and his desire to share God's comfort with others.

There then follows a narration (1:8–2:13), introduced by the characteristic narrative word *gar* (1:8) and describing briefly, and with probability, as a narration should, the circumstances in which Paul has found himself since he last communicated with the Corinthians. A narration should also be clear, which is not exactly the case here, but of course the Corinthians knew more about the situation than we do.

Woven into the narration are passages which reveal Paul's defense against charges made against him. In the first part (1:8–11) Paul is clearly seeking the personal sympathy of the Corinthians, and ethos is thus combined with pathos, but in verse 12 he takes a more positive tone and asserts that his actions have been right. In verses 13–14 it emerges that the specific question involves a letter he has written to the Corinthians. He does not deny the fact of his having written such a letter or argue about their understanding of the terms in which it was couched. Thus his defense will not be made on stasis of fact or of definition.

In verse 15 he resumes his narrative account, strengthens his ethos as a reasonable man by seeming to debate with himself about his intentions (17–18), denies that he is "worldly," and asserts that he honestly wanted to visit Corinth. He has acted as God would have him act, and his ethos is strengthened by identification of himself and the Corinthians together in God and Christ. In verse 23 he reveals the basis of his defense: "it was to spare you that I refrained from coming to Corinth." This is stasis of quality, specifically that form of it known as *antistasis*, in which a speaker claims that an advantage has resulted from his action. The letter he wrote to the Corinthians, which they appear to have found so offensive, was written out of love: "For I wrote you out of much affliction and anguish of heart and with many tears, not to cause you pain but to let you know the abundant love that I have for you" (2:4). It would thus appear that the charge was that he had refused to go to Corinth and instead had written an angry letter to the Corinthians.

In the following passage he justifies the letter as a test of their obedience (2:9) and he seeks to transfer the responsibility for the pain to someone else (2:5) who has been motivated by Satan (2:11). Transference of responsibility is called *metastasis* and is another subdivision of stasis of quality. Here its chief function seems to be ethical: to allow Paul to forgive the guilty one (2:10). The narration then concludes with the remaining events which brought Paul to Macedonia, from where he is writing (2:12–13).

In 2:14–17 Paul states his proposition and makes a partition of the elements which will provide his proof. He enunciates the matter first as a metaphor, then more logically. Paul is the aroma of Christ to God bringing fragrance to those who are being saved and those who are perishing (2:14–15): "For we are not, like so many, peddlars of God's word; but (A) as men of sincerity, (B) as commissioned by God, (C) in the sight of God we speak in Christ" (2:17). Three headings are identified here which are taken up in what follows. Before doing so, however, Paul provides his character witnesses, as a defendant in court might do. The Corinthians themselves will be his letter of recommendation (3:1–3).

Then comes the proof, "working out" the headings of 2:17. This is done in an interlocked order (*synchysis*) which may be outlined thus:

B   "as commissioned by God" 3:4–4:1
A   "as men of sincerity" 4:2–6
B   "as commissioned by God" 4:7–12
A   "as men of sincerity" 4:13–5:10
C   "in the sight of God we speak in Christ" 5:11–6:13

Throughout the proof Paul repeatedly builds on the three topics we identified in his proem: God's mercy, his own afflictions, and his desire to share God's comfort with the Corinthians. It might be said that these topics provide the energy or impulse for action which is then carried out in the three positive roles identified by the headings. Paul's afflictions give pathos to the proof; his sincerity and his divine commission supply the ethos; the logos, required for one who would "speak in Christ," is embodied in enthymemes and examples. External evidence is supplied by the witness of the Corinthians (3:1–3) and occasional citation of texts from Scripture.

The divine commission is first developed in the passage from 3:4 to 4:1: "our competence is from God, who has made us competent to be ministers of a new covenant, not in a written code but in the Spirit" (3:5–6). The apostle here utilizes an adaptation of the "legal question" of rhetorical theory involving the letter and intent (spirit) of the law. He then amplifies it with a *synkrisis*, a comparison between the dispensation of Moses and that of Christ (3:7–18). (Synkrisis was one of the exercises practiced in rhetorical schools and is found most commonly in epideictic, but occasionally in other oratorical species.) The topic of the more and the less is employed: "If the dispensation of death . . . came with such splendor that the Israelites could not look at Moses' face . . . , will not the dispensation of the Spirit be attended with greater splendor?" (3:7–8). The idea is played with in various forms in the following verses, and the imagery of dark and light carried on all the way through 4:6. The section from 3:12 through 4:1

is an elaborate piece of reasoning in which various premises are stated and given some support, and a final conclusion drawn. It resembles an epichiereme, a fully stated rhetorical argument, rather than an enthymeme, in which a premise is only implied.

In 4:2 Paul suddenly takes up the heading of his sincerity, refines it (*expolitio*; see *Rhetoric to Herennius* 4.54–58), and applies the imagery of light to it (4:6). Then he returns to his divine commission (7–12), amplifying it by contrast with the topic of his own afflictions. The benefits of all of this accrue to the Corinthians, "so death is at work in us, but life in you" (12). Then he resumes the heading of sincerity, but this time in terms of faith and belief and the comfort that comes from them (4:13–5:10). Paul's own afflictions again provide a setting in which the value of that belief is amplified; the result is heightened pathos.

Verse 5:11 begins "Therefore, knowing the fear of the Lord, we persuade men." This is the heading "we speak in Christ" found in the partition of 2:17, which has so far not been given specific treatment. It is of course related to the divine commission, but differs in focusing specifically on the preaching and letter-writing role of the apostle, rather than on the basis of his authority. What Paul preaches is Christ crucified and risen, the kerygma, which is briefly summarized in 5:14–15. Paul's mission is "refined" through consideration of his personal experience (5:16–19) and leads to the conclusion "So we are ambassadors for Christ, God making his appeal through us," which becomes the basis of an appeal: "We beseech you on behalf of Christ, be reconciled to God" (20).

In the first thirteen verses of chapter 6 this appeal, still in the context of Paul's ministry, is given pathetic amplification in a highly characteristic style by the cumulation of a series of words which seem to come pouring out of his heart: "We put no obstacle in any one's way, so that no fault may be found with our ministry, but as servants of God we commend ourselves in every way: through great endurance, in afflictions, hardships, calamities, beatings, imprisonments, tumults, labors, watching, hunger; by purity, knowledge, forbearance, kindness, the Holy Spirit, genuine love, truthful speech, and the power of God, . . ." (6:3–7). In modern times this technique is known as *pleonasm*, a term derived from the late Greek rhetorician Phoebammon; in the *Rhetoric to Herennius* (4.52) it is the figure of thought *frequentatio*, and in Quintilian (8.4.27) it is called *synathroismos*. In writing it appears somewhat bizarre, but employed orally it draws a great deal of dramatic power from the variety of images it evokes and from the rhythmical force of the phrases, which are often emphasized by anaphora and homoeoteleuton. (It might be noted that the English translators of the Bible seek to give the list more grammatical variety than does Paul's Greek.) Verses 8–10 continue the pleonasm, but add to it paradox, which is a basic quality of Christian thought: "as unknown, and yet well known; as dying and behold we live; . . . as having nothing, and yet possessing everything." Paul himself in verse 11 describes what he has just performed: "Our mouth is open to you, Corinthians; our heart is wide." "Widen your hearts also" (6:13).

Verses 6:14–7:1 appear to be an interpolation. The rest of chapter 7 is an epilogue which recapitulates Paul's defense (7:2), rounds out the letter by completing the narrative of Paul's experience since arriving in Macedonia (7:5–7), builds on the three topics of the proem, and projects the pathos of Paul's afflictions onto the Corinthians with a considerable amount of pleonasm. The letter is rhetorically complete at this point. All of its topics and headings have been fully explored, and the end has been linked to the beginning.

Chapters 8 and 9 appear to be a complete rhetorical unit of the deliberative species, seeking a contribution for the relief of the Jerusalem church. It begins with an address, "brethren," concludes with thanks, and has its own internal rhetorical structure. The narrative of the generosity of the Macedonian church (8:1–6) sets an example for the Corinthians. Paul then prepares the ground (verses 8–9) for his proposition: "It is best for you now to complete what a year ago you began not only to do but to desire, so that your readiness in desiring it may be matched by your completing it out of what you have" (10–11). Reasons why the Corinthians should accede are enthymematically presented (12–14) and supported (15) by a quotation from Exodus. Verses 8:16–24 are a recommendation of Titus, who will act as Paul's agent in the collection; 9:1–5 explain why Paul writes at this particular time. The rest of chapter 9 is an epilogue which recapitulates the request, supports it with argument and citation of Scripture, and heightens the emotional tone.

Can chapters 8 and 9 possibly be part of the same letter as chapters 1–7? The juxtaposition of the two blocks of text is rhetorically unsatisfactory: 1–7 is too long to serve as an introduction to 8–9, and yet 8–9 is too developed to be a kind of postscript to 1–7. (That Paul wrote approximations of postscripts can be seen in 1 Corinthians 16, but that chapter consists of a series of short admonitions which do not overbalance the letter as a whole.) Chapters 8–9 were certainly sent to Corinth by Titus (8:17–18), and it is possible that Titus was entrusted with both letters but instructed to deliver 1–7 first and allow its good effects to be felt before presenting 8–9. An objection against this, however, is the tone of 7:15, which seems to imply that Titus is still with Paul in Macedonia. Paul does not consistently indicate in a letter who is its bearer—not in 1 Corinthians, for example—and it thus remains possible that 1–7 was sent in advance of Titus' trip. Probably the Corinthians kept Paul's letters together in a roll box, and when requests for copies were received from other churches, all the material now found in 2 Corinthians was copied onto one papyrus roll. It would be more convenient to send in that form. A closure of 1–7, a salutation and closure of 8–9, and salutation of 10–13 were probably omitted in making such copies, for otherwise they would be preserved in some version of the text.

Chapters 10–13 have often been regarded as the original letter which caused so much distress in Corinth and which Paul claims he both regretted and did not regret, for it brought the Corinthians to repentance, though at some cost (7:8). It was probably preserved with the letter of 1–7, as an appendix to explain it. The rhetorical species of 2 Corinthians 10–13 is clearly judicial: Paul admits that he is making an apology (12:19). The "indictment" he is answering can be summed up in the quotation at 10:10: "For they say, 'His letters are weighty and strong, but his bodily presence is weak, and his speech of no account.'" But there is more to it than that, for Paul's authority as an apostle seems to have been questioned by opponents in Corinth on many counts, and these criticisms have to be reconstructed from his oblique allusions. Interpretation is complicated by the tone, which is sometimes ironic (as in 10:1 and 11:1), but there are passages of disarming candor as well (as 11:5). Few chapters in the epistles better illustrate the complexity of Paul's mind. The narrative of Paul's sufferings for his faith (11:22–29), amplified by pleonasm, was used by Augustine (*On Christian Doctrine* 4.12) to prove that true eloquence, even by classical standards, could be found in the Scriptures.

Second Corinthians 10–13 is of great rhetorical interest because it shows Paul's consciousness, and his manipulation, of two different kinds of rhetoric, the radical (basically sacred) rhetoric of authority and the rhetoric of rational argumentation, which was perceived as more worldly. It is possible that the clash of these two ways of enunciating the faith and the irony in which they are here held in tension are part of the reason that the letter was so disturbing to some at Corinth; it would seem that Paul did not fit their notion of what an apostle should be. His personality seemed to change radically from one time to another. The tension is immediately evident in the opening verses of chapter 10. Paul first entreats the Corinthians by the meekness and gentleness of Christ, but then immediately recasts an objection made against him by ironically asserting it: "I who am humble when face to face with you, but bold to you when away!" "Humble" is one of several words used in the letter to refer to the Pauline adaptation of radical Christian rhetoric: that intuitive grasp of sacred language which makes no pretence to the devices of art and secures its authority from simple directness of faith and works. Although assertive, it is characterized by gentleness and modesty, and the personality of the speaker is almost totally eclipsed by the message. Paul had sought to practice this at Corinth; but at a distance, his critics charge, he inconsistently assumes all the weapons of the orator and thunders against them in pleonastic, highly personal outpourings.

"Humble" in 2 Corinthians 10:1 is the "not worldly" of 10:3, but Paul defines two kinds of "boldness," a distinction made most clearly in 11:17, where he contrasts boasting with the Lord's authority on the one hand with boasting of worldly things on the other. The latter rhetorical technique is illustrated by the rest of chapter 11, where he passionately and eloquently boasts of his personal sufferings, "the things that show my weakness." In contrast, the boldness claimed in chapter 10 is that of the Lord's authority: "The weapons of our warfare are not worldly but have divine power to destroy strongholds" (10:4). This kind of boldness is forced on Paul, he claims, by the need to refute attacks upon himself and his gospel. Refutation involves argumentation, and it is aggressive and often harsh in tone and personal. Paul goes on to admit that "we destroy arguments" (*logismoi*), the regular term for reasoning in Aristotle. He has earlier pleaded with the Corinthians not to put him in a position of having to address them in the terms he has felt compelled to use with others (10:2).

This then is the inconsistency which was perceived in him, his inclination to testify to the faith gently, humbly, experientially, and intuitively, but when thwarted or attacked to refute others' arguments with all the weapons of dialectic and rhetoric. In the latter process his personality emerged as sometimes dominant, sometimes defensive. The power for both humble testimony and dialectical refutation, Paul claims, despite their difference in style, comes from the same source, from God: "Let such people understand that what we say by letter when absent, we do when present" (10:11). He acknowledges the power of speech, which derives from Christ and is manifested not only in preaching the gospel, but also where necessary in resisting evil: "If I come again I will not spare them [his opponents in Corinth]—since you desire proof that Christ is speaking in me" (13:2).

Paul had been criticized as "of no account" in speech. This he affects to grant: "If I am unskilled in speaking, I am not in knowledge" (11:6). In the Greek, "unskilled" is a noun, *idiotes*, which basically denotes a private person, not a professional; it does not rule out the individual's informal acquaintance with a subject or practice in it. Paul apparently felt that the knowledge of which he speaks furnished him a skill in speaking on those occasions when it was needed—for example, when his apostolic authority was attacked. Then he spoke not as a private person, but with the Lord's authority. Both here and in 1 Corinthians, Paul represents the knowledge (*gnosis*) which he has as "foolishness" in the eyes of the world. It is a knowledge obtained by personal religious experience, as in his own conversion or the experience of the man caught up to the third heaven, which is described in 2 Corinthians 12:2–4. The latter heard "things that cannot be told, which man may not utter." There is thus some secret knowledge, a Christian gnosticism.

Paul's account of Christian rhetoric in 2 Corinthians can be amplified somewhat by what he had said in the opening chapters of 1 Corinthians, with its celebrated working out of the paradox of Christian knowledge as the foolishness of the world. The function of the passage there was to supply the authority needed for his specific (deliberative) injunctions to the Corinthians in succeeding chapters. Speech, he says (1 Cor. 1:5–7), is a spiritual gift. Christ has sent him to preach the gospel, "and not with eloquent wisdom, lest the cross of Christ be emptied of its power" (verse 17). This he explains to mean that the word of the cross seems folly to those who are perishing, "but to us who are being saved it is the power of God" (18). The debater of this age is nothing (20). "Jews demand signs and Greeks seek wisdom, but we preach Christ crucified" (22–23). Thus when Paul first came to the Corinthians he did not proclaim "the testimony of God in lofty words of wisdom" (2:1). His speech and message were not in plausible words, but were a demonstration of power (4), and what he imparts through them is "a secret and hidden wisdom of God" (7). Even the words themselves are "not taught by human wisdom but taught by the Spirit" (13). When he first came to Corinth, he says, he had to feed the Corinthians "with milk, not with solid food" (3:2). This seems to imply some rhetorical strategy of making his doctrine initially appealing, or at least simple, and even so he claims the Corinthians were not ready for it. All this seems consistent with the "humble" style described in 2 Corinthians, but it makes no provision for the "bold" style to which Paul will later feel himself pushed, and which he will acknowledge, in 2 Corinthians.

Paul was a complex person of conflicting personality traits which he sought to control through religious discipline. In 2 Corinthians that effort at control becomes evident. There are two aspects of personality and thus two rhetorics in tension in his writings. One has worldly characteristics and is seen in his understanding of the forms of logical argument and refutation, in deliberate arrangement of material, and in careful choice and composition of words. This is evoked in reaction to others and is often characterized by a tone of anger, as in 2 Corinthians 10–13 and in Galatians. The radical rhetoric which Paul more willingly acknowledges is something external to himself, characterized by authority, power, and direct illumination, and its mode of expression is gentler, though in Paul's case perhaps a constrained gentleness. This tension of gentleness and anger in Christian rhetoric is doubtless a reflection of the tension between the God of anger and justice and the God of love and mercy in Christian theology. Jesus too both preached and practiced radical rhetoric; but to judge from the Gospels, gentleness was natural to him, anger constrained, and he was the master of something Paul did not control, the directly illuminating parable. As it turned out, none of these rhetorical forms would be adequate for the mission of the Church in the next few centuries; the initial energy of Christianity was dissipated by historical experience, above all by the failure of the age to end, and the second century saw the development of new and more worldly forms of preaching.

Chapter Five. The Rhetoric of the Gospels

The canon of the New Testament was established by Councils of the Church in late antiquity. Whether consciously determined or not, the order assigned to the books is interesting, for it is consistent with conventions of rhetoric as taught in the schools. First come the Gospels, which proclaim the message; then the narrative of Acts, which describes its reception; then the epistles, which may be viewed as arguing out interpretations of the message; and finally the Apocalypse, as a dramatic epilogue. The order of the four Gospels probably reflects what the Church thought was the chronological order of their composition and is consistent with Eusebius' reports on that subject. But it is also rhetorically effective in that Matthew, with his introductory genealogy, account of Jesus' birth, and extended speeches, gives a comprehensive initial picture of Christianity and links it to the Old Testament; Mark, with his emphasis on what Jesus did, approximates a narration; Luke works out details and smoothes over problems to create a plausible whole; and John supplies a moving epilogue. Finally, the arrangement of each Gospel tends toward an oratorical structure. Each has some kind of proem, some narration of events, if not of the early life of Jesus, at least of the beginnings of his ministry in the encounter with John the Baptist, an exposition of his teaching leading to an account of the crucifixion, and the joyful resurrection as epilogue. Discussion of the genre of the Gospels is irrelevant to our purpose—only Luke shows any awareness of classical genre—in that all genres are rhetorical: they are attempts to find a structure and a style which will accomplish the objectives of the author. In terms of the theory of four kinds or levels of style set forth in Demetrius' treatise *On Style*, Mark may be said to adopt the plain style, Luke the elegant style, John the elevated style, and Matthew the forceful style. A classical rhetorician probably would have regarded all four Gospels as lacking literary merit, with the possible exception of some passages in Luke or John, but Augustine and other Christians came to see that such judgments result from a rather arbitrary definition of grammatical, rather than rhetorical, standards.

The rhetorical unit of each Gospel can be taken to be the received text, though there are of course some doubtful passages such as the two endings of Mark, and John 7:53–8:11. The rhetorical situation must be specified separately for each Gospel, in terms of the audience to which it is addressed. Matthew appears to be addressed to a Jewish audience familiar with the law and the Scriptures, probably at least partially converted to Christianity but needing a fuller statement of the relationship of the new faith to the older tradition. It is sometimes thought that his work is addressed to catechumens. Mark is seemingly addressed to devout Christians who want a written account of the sayings and deeds of Jesus in simple terms that they can understand and use in their life and worship. Luke expressly writes (1:1–4) for the converted, supplying additional details of the story of Christ, and in contrast to Matthew addresses an audience including gentiles. John states (20:31) that he writes to convert; thus he apparently hoped for some readers not yet Christian, or perhaps more accurately, not fully acknowledging Christ in the terms understood by himself, but he may also have sought to provide a community of which he was a part with a justification for their special view of Christianity.

Because of their differences in purpose and in audience, the rhetorical problems of the evangelists differ. They do, however, in different ways, address four great rhetorical problems of biblical Christianity which have continued to be major objections to the Christian faith. The first of these is that the Jews, and especially the Jewish religious establishment of Palestine, despite expectation of a Messiah, did not accept Jesus as that Messiah (nor do they two thousand years later). Matthew in particular grapples with this problem, but it can be found in the other Gospels as well. The general approach taken is to stress the fact that Jewish prophecy itself included statements indicating that the Messiah would not be received by his own people. This explanation bred serious philosophical problems in that it perpetuated in Christian theology an arbitrary quality in God which might seem inconsistent with the definition of him as creator of all things and source of light, life, and love. But the evangelists, with the partial exception of John, are not philosophers, and they and their audience accepted a polarization of those who were saved and those who were lost. It was endemic to the world as they saw it.

A second problem for biblical Christianity was that the end of the age prophesied by Jesus as soon to occur had not taken place a generation after Jesus' death, at least not in the terms in which he seems to describe it. The most vivid treatment of the issue is that given in Mark 13, which stands out in contrast to Mark's usual style in reporting the sayings of Jesus. The passage is cast specifically in terms of the coming destruction of the temple, an event which of course did take place at the hands of the Romans in A.D. 70 and which may have been anticipated, unless the passage is a later addition to the Gospel reflecting knowledge of the fact. But Mark 13 ends by stressing that the time of cataclysm is unknown; Christians must simply keep watch. Luke seems to push the event off to a distant future time; John stresses eschatology as realized in the present.

A third problem, for a modern audience, is the lack of historical verification of the Gospel account. In the famous words of Edward Gibbon, "Under the reign of Tiberius, the whole earth, or at least a celebrated province of the Roman empire, was involved in a preternatural darkness of three hours. Even this miraculous event, which ought to have excited the wonder, the curiosity, and the devotion of mankind, passed without notice in an age of science and history" (*Decline and Fall of the Roman Empire*, chapter 15, *ad finem*). Matthew, Mark, and John almost completely ignore this problem, which did not concern their audiences. To them Christianity is something directly and personally experienced which requires no outside confirmation other than that found in Jewish prophecy. Luke (23:44–45) reports the three hours of darkness without comment, allowing it to contribute to the pathetic effect of the crucifixion; but earlier he has sought to link the events he describes to contemporary history by giving dates and carefully naming public officials. He alone, for example, notes (23:6–7) that Jesus of Galilee was legally under the jurisdiction of Herod and not that of Pilate. This concern with historical detail contributes a sense of veracity to his account.

Finally, there is the problem that though Jesus may have been an inspired prophet, a charismatic teacher, a healer of the sick, even a miracle worker, other such figures were not unknown in his time—Apollonius of Tyana being one example—and the crucial question is whether he was in any literal, special sense *the* Son of the Father and God. The approach of the synoptic Gospels to this problem is to establish Jesus' authority through prophecy, signs, and witnesses, then to portray him as asserting divinity, and to give the concept a final meaning in the account of the resurrection. It is interesting, however, how little evidence for the resurrection they provide, especially in contrast to their initial efforts to establish Jesus' authority. In the shorter text of Mark, often thought to be the original version, there are no human witnesses at all to the resurrection. Matthew, rather defensively, tells the story that the guard at the tomb was bribed to say that the disciples had taken away the body and adds that this was commonly believed among the Jews (28:11–15). Even when the disciples saw the risen Jesus, "some doubted" (28:17), and their reaction to Jesus' final words is not reported. That the account in Mark was perceived to be rhetorically weak can be seen in the efforts of Luke to improve upon it. Both in his Gospel and in the opening chapter of Acts, he seeks verisimilitude by supplying additional detail. John, who directly tackles the problem of the divinity of Christ in his opening verses and throughout his

Gospel, provides the most powerful epilogue, especially the striking story of Thomas (20:24–29) and the fine concluding chapter on the encounter of Peter and the beloved disciple with the Lord. He seems to be saying that the evidence for the resurrection is not to be found in the multiplication of witnesses, but in the depth of personal experience of those who acknowledge it.

In meeting their rhetorical problems the evangelists had certain things to build upon which they fully exploit. These are first of all external evidence: the prophecies of the Old Testament fulfilled by Christ; the miracles performed by Jesus; and a considerable number of witnesses who could be cited, including John the Baptist, the disciples, some of whom came to be well known eventually, and other people who could be named. Their strongest internal evidence was probably the pathos inherent in Jesus' life, suffering, and resurrection, in the appeal of his character (an internal ethos complementing his authority), and in the doctrines of faith, hope, and love which they could teach. They had something to say which they knew their readers longed to hear and which had a mythopoeic force. Pharisaical opposition could be turned to advantage in that it could arouse sympathy and understanding for Jesus. Jesus' rejection of and by the world was an experience in which many of their readers could share. These points, therefore, could be effectively developed. Finally, the external evidence could be used as the basis for artistic argument, which could give a logical coherence to the account for those in the audience who appreciated it. In a word, the evangelists could solve their rhetorical problems by a careful use of ethos, pathos, and logos, in that order of priority.

The rhetorical characteristics of the Gospels are established in their opening chapters. Let us look at each briefly.

Of the four Gospels, Matthew's makes the widest use of all aspects of rhetoric. He arranges his Gospel into distinct parts which perform specific rhetorical functions, and he is con-

cerned not only to establish the ethos of Jesus' authority and
the pathos of his suffering, but consistently to provide his
readers with something close to logical argument. He appears
to furnish reason to make what is said seem probable and to
allow his audience to feel some intellectual security in his account. This audience was certainly Jewish and familiar with
the Scriptures. Matthew's careful efforts at proof might reflect doubts in his audience that Jesus was the Messiah, but
could also result from an intention to supply a work for catechumens.

Matthew begins with a clearly defined proem (1:1–17). It is
an unusual proem which makes no specific appeal to the interest and sympathy of the audience, but it nevertheless performs
that function. In the first verse he identifies Jesus as the son of
David, the son of Abraham. These two names immediately
attract the reader's attention and mark the subject as important. They also lay the basis for the repeated references to the
fulfillment of prophecy in what will follow and for the authoritative ethos of Jesus. It is characteristic of Matthew that he is
not content simply to assert the essential fact of Jesus' genealogy, but insists on "proving" it. This he does by reciting in
verses 2–16 the entire genealogy. The list is commonly regarded as apologetic or polemical and as explicitly addressed to
an audience which expected a Messiah from the house of David rather than from some other source. (The matter is well
discussed by Marshall D. Johnson in *The Purpose of the Biblical
Genealogies*.) There is probably some element of personal appeal present as well, for some of his readers would regard
themselves as descended from or connected with individuals
named in the genealogy. As if this were not enough, Matthew
then organizes the genealogy into three groups in verse 17:
fourteen generations from Abraham to David, fourteen from
David to the Babylonian captivity, and fourteen from the Babylonian captivity to Jesus. The numerology shows that we have
arrived at a very important point in history, well worthy of our
attention.

Then come the stories of Jesus' birth, his encounter with

John the Baptist, his temptation, his gathering of the disciples, and his first miracles. Together these function as a narration and set the stage for the proposition, Jesus' teaching in the Sermon on the Mount, but each also provides an important testimony of external evidence to establish the authoritative ethos of Jesus. We are shown that Jesus must be the Messiah because (1) his birth fulfilled the prophecy of the birth of the Messiah, (2) he was so acclaimed by John the Baptist, (3) he was so recognized by God, (4) he was tested and proved true by the devil, (5) the disciples immediately responded to his call, and (6) he could heal the sick. Taken together with the genealogy, these episodes provide documentary evidence, witnesses, and signs, major forms of external proof. Herod is introduced as a witness, for he recognizes the fulfillment of the prophecy of the Messiah and proves it by his grand-scale efforts to kill the child. That the disciples are witnesses to Jesus is seen in their immediate response to his call; they do not have to be persuaded, but intuitively recognize him. It is worth comparing Matthew's account of Jesus' meeting with John the Baptist to that in Mark; Mark does not give the crucial words that make John a witness to Jesus: "I need to be baptized by you and do you come to me?" (Matthew 3:14).

Matthew also employs the internal proof of logical argument. He himself does not reason about the truth of what he presents, but the characters involved, including Jesus, do. He has them speak in enthymemes: they regularly support an assertion with a reason which helps to make it more comprehensible. The first enthymeme in Matthew occurs in the words of the angel to Joseph: "Do not fear to take Mary your wife, for that which is conceived in her is of the Holy Spirit" (1:20). This is immediately followed by a second enthymeme, explaining why the savior is to be called Jesus. This is a logical angel who wants Joseph to understand and is not content simply to make authoritative announcements. Similarly, the magi explain to Herod why they have come (2:2), the priests and scribes explain to Herod how they know that Jesus will be born in Bethlehem (2:5), the angel explains to Joseph why he should flee into Egypt (2:13) and again why he should leave (2:20), John the Baptist gives a reason why the people should repent (3:2), the devil explains to Jesus why he can safely throw himself down from the pinnacle of the temple (4:6), and finally Jesus himself repeats the enthymeme of John, "Repent, for the kingdom of heaven is at hand" (4:17). For all its miraculous events, Matthew's world is far more rational than that described by Mark, who has little interest in such things. In many cases, the minor premise of the enthymeme is a scriptural quotation. The external evidence, which functions cumulatively to show that prophecy has been fulfilled in the birth of Jesus, is thus utilized to construct an argument internal to the text.

Once having established the ethical and logical basis of his narrative in chapters 1–4, Matthew can now proceed to an exposition of Jesus' teaching, which he does dramatically in the Sermon on the Mount. This can be said to function as a proposition for his Gospel as a whole. In terms of Matthew's rhetoric, its most important features are emphasis on the law, extensive use of enthymemes, and hostility to gentiles. Jesus' eschatology is implicit in what he says, but not clearly expounded to the crowd. Though the sermon fits well into Matthew's rhetoric, it does not follow that it is totally his creation. As John later points out (21:25), there was much that could be said about Jesus. Individual evangelists chose the material which most suited their needs.

The Gospel of Mark is an example of what may be called radical Christian rhetoric, a form of "sacred language" characterized by assertion and absolute claims of authoritative truth without evidence or logical argument. According to Eusebius (*Church History* 2.15), the Gospel of Mark originated in the request of Christian communities founded by Saint Peter to have a written account of the gospel to read when the apostle moved on to a new locality. This is not unlikely, for it is clear from the outset that Mark is addressing convinced Christians.

If the words "the Son of God" appearing in his first verse are genuine (the Greek text is in doubt), he simply asserts who Jesus is. In verses 2–3 he cites the prophecy of the coming of John, but otherwise in his opening chapters ignores the need Matthew felt for evidence from Scripture. His picture of John the Baptist is that of a prophet who asserts his vision, take it or leave it. In 1:11 God authoritatively proclaims who Jesus is. The temptation by Satan is given as a fact but not utilized to prove anything. When Jesus begins to preach, his message is cast not as an enthymeme, not, as in Matthew, "Repent, for the kingdom of heaven is at hand," but as four authoritative assertions: "The time is fulfilled, and the kingdom of God is at hand; repent, and believe in the gospel" (1:15). This is followed by the authoritative calling of the disciples, who immediately respond. "Immediately" is one of Mark's favorite words and gives a forward movement to his account. The truth is immediately and intuitively apprehended because it is true. Some see it, others do not, but there is no point in trying to persuade the latter. This is the most radical form of Christian rhetoric. When Jesus performs his first miracle, the witnesses are "amazed" (1:27); they recognize truth but do not comprehend it rationally. The miracle is a sign of authority, as the crowd at once admits. No effort is made to include any picture of Jesus' early teaching as seen in the Sermon on the Mount and the Sermon on the Plain. This kind of explanation is irrelevant to Mark. When Jesus preaches in Mark it is in parables, which are directly apprehended.

There are enthymemes in Mark, but they are usually of a very simple sort, offering an obvious explanation and usually in his own voice. Simon and Andrew are casting nets, "for they were fishermen" (1:16). Many tax collectors and sinners are seated with Jesus, "for there were many who followed him" (2:15). Even Jesus in Mark occasionally uses such simple explanations: "Let us go on to the next towns, that I may preach there also; for that is why I came out" (1:38). In the parables, Jesus is of course employing an inductive method, and Mark, like other evangelists, shows him applying the law of contradictories: "No one sews a piece of unshrunk cloth on an old garment; if he does, the patch tears away from it, the new from the old, and a worse tear is made" (2:21). In the opening chapters of Mark the enthymeme which carries the greatest rhetorical force is that in which Mark explains why those in the synagogue at Capernaum were astonished at Jesus' teaching: "for he taught them as one who had authority, and not as the scribes" (1:22). The same enthymeme occurs in the same context in Luke (4:31–32), who doubtless took it from Mark. It appears in Matthew as well, but in a different context (7:29). This may mean that it was a commonplace used to describe reaction to Jesus and that its form is not specifically attributable to Mark. He is not attracted to it by its form, but because of its content: its picture of direct reaction to Jesus' power.

The question is likely to be asked whether rhetorical analysis can determine which Gospel, that of Matthew or that of Mark, is prior in composition and which evangelist may have used the other's work. Rhetorically it seems very unlikely that Mark could have used Matthew's account. That hypothesis requires the assumption that Mark read the Gospel of Matthew and reacted strongly against its rhetoric. He would then have composed his own version, using material from Matthew, but stripping it of its argumentation and amplification, and restoring the gospel to that radical rhetoric which he regarded as more genuine. There is no good model for that kind of redaction elsewhere; it is inconsistent with the traditions of the early Church about the origins of the Gospels, as preserved by Eusebius. And such a negative attitude toward his source might well have impelled Mark to write a preface warning readers to beware of the false tradition, or even have led him to distrust the wording of Matthew at every turn. All of this seems psychologically improbable, and thus Mark very likely represents the survival of a continuous tradition of radical rhetoric in the early Church, long associated with the apostleship of Peter. Paul certainly knew this tradition, but his own work represents a modification of it in the direction of rationalizing. Presumably the gospel preached by Apollos and also by the docetists went even further in this direction.

That Matthew might have recast Mark's account into a more rationalizing rhetoric is a better possibility. If so, he was seeking to adapt the gospel to an audience which in this, as in other respects, thought in different ways or had different needs. For any among his readers familiar with Mark, the preservation of some similarities of expression would have been reassuring and have helped to authenticate his work.

Luke opens his Gospel with a fine periodic sentence, immediately reassuring to an educated speaker of Greek. His addressee is the unknown Theophilus, apparently a person of some influence (*kratiste*, 1:2) and bearing a Hellenized name. What Luke promises to provide is a version of the gospel which differs from the many others (*polloi*, 1:1) in existence by its orderly narrative (*kathexes*, 1:3) and its exactness of detail (*akribos*, 1:3; *asphaleian*, 1:4). He is writing for those already converted who want to know more. The words "that you may know the truth" (1:5) are somewhat misleading in the Revised Standard Version. Luke is not saying that other gospels are not true, only that he will follow a more rigorous narrative method and be more specific.

This purpose is immediately borne out by his account of the births of John the Baptist and Jesus. We are given names and dates and told exactly what was said. It is difficult not to view the dialogue as an invention of Luke himself. He identifies no sources. Was there really a surviving oral tradition of, for example, what Elizabeth said when she realized she had conceived? Probably, like a Greek historian or biographer, Luke sought to recreate in his own mind what she would have said. This amounts to prosopopoeia, the exercise of the rhetorical schools in which a historical or mythological character is imagined in some situation and his or her feelings expressed (the

Heroides of Ovid are poetic examples). In the Magnificat (1: 46–55), Luke has based his composition on Hannah's prayer in 1 Samuel 2:1–10. Luke's angels, like Matthew's, speak in enthymemes, but because they are more wordy and supply more detail, the enthymematic quality of their statements is less striking.

Since Luke appears to have used both Mark and a source common to Matthew, his rhetoric combines some of the qualities of each but mutes their tones. For example, he includes a genealogy of Joseph going all the way back to Adam (3:23–38), but unlike the genealogy in Matthew it performs little persuasive function in its context; it is part of his promise to provide detail and at most lends some historiographic credence to his overall narrative. Unlike the other evangelists, he claims to know something about Jesus' youth. His description of Jesus in the temple at the age of twelve (2:41–47) helps prepare the reader to understand Jesus' later skill in meeting the Pharisees. He amplifies Mark's account of the early period of Jesus' ministry with the Sermon on the Plain (6:20–49) and thus softens Mark's radical rhetoric, but he does not attribute to Jesus the emphasis on the law or the hostility to gentiles found in Matthew. In chapter 8 he also mutes the effect of both Matthew 13 and Mark 4. Luke is chiefly of interest here in that he shows what he thought would be meaningful to Christians a generation after Jesus' death: a more elegant presentation in better Greek, more biographical detail, and, as noted earlier, a fuller account of the period after the resurrection. Luke in the Gospel comes close to being a classical biographer, just as in Acts he comes close to being a classical historian.

The treatise *On Sublimity*, attributed to Longinus, identifies (section 8) five sources of *hypsos*, the quality of elevation or sublimity in great writing. The first and most important of these is the power to conceive great thoughts; second is strong, inspired emotion; the others are elevation in the use of figures, especially figures of thought, in the choice of diction, and in the arrangement of words. Examples are drawn largely from the classical Greek poets, Plato, and Demosthenes, but in one passage (9.9) the author cites "the lawgiver of the Jews, no ordinary man, since he worthily grasped and expressed the power of the divine when writing at the very outset of his work, 'God said,' he says, What? 'Let there be light, and there was; let there be earth, and there was.'" A Greek rhetorician who could see *hypsos* in Genesis could probably have caught a glimpse of it also in the Gospel of John, if he had known it.

John's elevated thought and style is evident from the first verse of his prologue, with its reminiscence of the opening of Genesis. It is not distinguished by figures of thought, but the other sources of *hypsos* can be identified: the conceptual power, the emotion, the diction, especially the metaphors, and the arrangement of the words, such as the chiasmus of the first verse.

John's prologue has some of the characteristics of a proem, more of a proposition. Nothing is told us about the author or his purpose in writing, but the passage attracts serious attention through its *hypsos* and its *emphasis*, which as we have noted earlier is a quality of seeming to mean much more than one says. Since the prologue can hardly be comprehended on first hearing, it is not a purely rhetorical composition. Many scholars regard it as a hymn sung in the community of which John was a member. John does not identify his audience, but one is implied in his choice of words: Hellenized Jews with some ability at abstract thought, familiar with the *memra*, or Old Testament word of God, and the *logos*, or divine reason of pagan philosophers, which had been taken up by Philo and other Jewish thinkers. It is these whom John would like to persuade or reassure that Jesus is to be identified with the *logos* and is the Son of God. Late in his Gospel (20:31) he clearly states that he writes to convert the nonbeliever.

Viewed as a proposition, the first fourteen verses set forth a sequence of at least five topics (they could be subdivided into a larger number), most of which are given development subsequently in the Gospel. These topics are a series of definitions: the Word was God; God was the creator; God is life; God is light; the Word was made flesh. The topics are authoritatively enunciated with no attempt at proof, though the topic of light is given some amplification in verses 5 and 9. The authoritative ethos must be said to derive from God and to be intuitively recognized, since the author does nothing to establish his own authority. This intuitive grasp of the divine is central to John's rhetoric, as may be seen in 1:12: "But to all who received him, who believed in his name, he gave power to become the children of God." Such a one is the evangelist himself.

Although modern editions usually begin a new paragraph at 1:14, this verse begins with a connective and by the conventions of Greek writing should go with the preceding verse. It is in fact the climax of a sequence which leads from the creation to the incarnation. Verse 15, oddly treated as a parenthesis in the Revised Standard Version, is the opening of a sequence of three passages which elaborate and thus support John's thought. Verses 15–18 demonstrate intuitive judgment, which is at the heart of the religious experience as John understands it; 19–28 demonstrate the evidence from prophecy, which substantiates this intuitive judgment; and 29–36 resume the intuitive judgment and confirm it with a sign. The passage as a whole provides the witness of John the Baptist to the Messiah; it is followed by the witness of the disciples. In Mark the witness of John the Baptist and the disciples is only implicit, and in Matthew it is explicit, but briefly treated among other evidence. In John it is fully exploited. John the Baptist and the disciples are here powerful character witnesses to the truth of the message and to the ethos of the evangelist.

If 1:6–8 is genuine (it seems rather intrusive), it is intended to anticipate the importance of John the Baptist as a witness. This is then taken up in the opening words of 1:15, "John bore witness to him." No scriptural prophecy is cited in John's recognition of Christ in the remainder of the verse, which is, however, cast as an enthymeme: "This was he of whom I said, 'He who comes after me ranks before me, for he was before me.'" The recognition is immediate and intuitive, and the mi-

nor premise of the enthymeme is an assertion of that fact. In
16–18 the evangelist then gives his commentary on John's proclamation, concluding with the words "No one has ever seen
God; the only Son, who is in the bosom of the Father, he has
made him known." The word for "made known" is *exegesato*,
related to English "exegesis." As the Father is known through
the Son, so both are known through the evangelist; but the
exegesis of each is based on revelation, on direct apprehen-
sion of truth. The evangelist's explanation is given as a series
of assertions, like those in the prologue, and there are no
enthymemes.

In 1:19 we are told again that this is the testimony of John
the Baptist. In confrontation with the priests and Levites he
reiterates his perception of Christ, but this time supports his
own role by scriptural citation, "as the prophet Isaiah said"
(1:23). Once the intuitive recognition is made, the truth of the
prophecy is understood.

In 1:29–34 John the Baptist again proclaims the recognition
and this time supports it with a sign, the vision of the Spirit
descending as a dove. Twice in the passage John says that he
"bears witness." The evangelist has placed this passage third in
the sequence of recognition, but verse 33 reveals that John had
earlier been prepared for the event. He remarks "I myself did
not know him, but he who sent me to baptize with water said
to me, 'He on whom you see the Spirit descend and remain,
this is he who baptizes with the Holy Spirit.'"

There follows the recognition by the disciples. It begins
(1:35) with a repetition of John's perception of the Lamb of
God, which provides an authority for the first two disciples,
but they immediately grasp an understanding and follow Jesus.
To none of the disciples does Jesus have to explain himself or
provide any teaching, and Nathaniel hails him spontaneously
as "the Son of God" (1:49). Conversation between Jesus and
the disciples is realistic, even humorous, which invigorates and
amplifies the seriousness of the underlying thought. The great
mysteries are cast in a very human situation. There is direct
rapport.

John 2–3 makes up a rhetorical unit which is framed by

incidents in Cana (2:1 and 4:46). Central position is given to a resumption of the testimony of John the Baptist (3:23–36), which is also framed by two incidents, the encounters with Nicodemus and the woman of Samaria. The most remarkable feature of this section is that although it corresponds to the account of the beginning of Jesus' ministry in the synoptic Gospels, it contains no mention whatsoever of Jesus' preaching in synagogues or speaking to crowds or engaging in any systematic exposition of his message: "Many believed in his name when they saw the signs which he did; but Jesus did not trust himself to them, because he knew all men and needed no one to bear witness of man; for he himself knew what was in man" (2:23–25). The main function of the passage is to demonstrate the signs, to present additional witnesses, and to allow exegesis of the evangelist's understanding of the significance of the events. This occurs in 2:11: "This, the first of his signs, Jesus did at Cana in Galilee, and manifested his glory; and his disciples believed in him." The editorializing in 2:17 and 2:22 involves a recognition of the meaning of Scripture. Verses 3:16–21 and 3:31–36 are probably also editorializing by the evangelist in his characteristic assertive thought and choice of word.

Finally, in the long discourse of chapter 5, the evangelist presents an exposition of theology by Jesus. Presumably he thought that by this point the reader would have apprehended the ethos of Jesus and would be ready for a more extended exploration of his thought. The discourse of 5:19–47 is thus John's equivalent of the Sermon on the Mount—but rhetorically it differs radically. The scene occurs at Jerusalem in a direct encounter with "the Jews." Jesus' eschatology is made more explicit (5:25–29) than in Matthew. Nothing is said about the law, no commandments are given, no parables told. The technique is amplification of a small number of topics. At least two are identical to topics developed again in chapters 13–17, the relationship of the Son to the Father and the function of love, and they are in fact amplifications of the definitions in John's prologue. The imagery of light and darkness in the prologue is taken up as well. Proof is offered in the citation of the witness of John the Baptist (5:33), in the works which Jesus does (5:36), and in the evidence of Scripture (5:39), and the working out of the topics often takes the form of enthymemes. The speech ends with an indictment of the Jews, that is, of the Jewish religious establishment, which is given the authority of Moses (5:45–47): "Do not think that I shall accuse you to the Father; it is Moses who accuses you, on whom you set your hope." Then a hypothetical enthymeme: "If you believed Moses, you would believe me, for he wrote of me." Then its converse, turned into a rhetorical question: "But if you do not believe his writings, how will you believe my words?" The formal topic of the more and the less underlies this. If the Jews cannot understand the written words of Scripture, which are less difficult to perceive, how can they recognize the greater reality of the Son of God?

John's Gospel is radical Christian rhetoric in its demand for immediate and direct response to the truth, but John makes far more demands than Mark on his readers in approaching the truth they are to perceive. He uses the forms of logical argument not so much as proof, as does Matthew, but as ways of turning and reiterating the topics which are at the core of his message. Like Luke, he supplies a fuller version of the gospel, but fuller in the sense of a deeper perception of the kerygma rather than a linear expansion of the contents.

Chapter Six. The Speeches in Acts

The book of Acts resembles a classical historical monograph; it has a preface and consists of a chronological narrative into which speeches and a letter are inserted, as in the work of Greek historians. Luke's choice of this form suggests that he expects an audience with some education, who would appreciate it, and that he thinks of himself in the role of a Greek historian—not a scientific collector of facts, but an interpreter and dramatizer of the direction and meaning of events.

The historicity of speeches in Greek historians varies considerably from writer to writer. Some speeches in Polybius may be quite close to what was actually said. Thucydides (1.22) describes his own method in composing speeches, but scholars differ over how his words and practice should be understood. Many Greek historians in Roman imperial times (Dionysius of Halicarnassus, for example) clearly felt almost complete freedom in composing speeches, a task for which they had been given training and encouragement by exercises in the rhetorical schools. Eusebius and later church historians abandon the use of speeches, thus tacitly admitting that they were perceived as artificial.

All of this, as well as the existence of prosopopoeiae in Luke's Gospel, suggest that he would have felt free to compose speeches for participants in the events described in Acts on the basis of what they were likely to have said. What was "likely" was determined by the demands of the situation, the character and beliefs associated with the speaker in Luke's mind, the rhetorical conventions of the setting, and what would seem appropriate to Luke's readers. If he knew, or thought he knew, the actual argument used on the occasion or on a similar occasion, that too would be a factor. Beginning in chapter 20 he either reports his own firsthand witness of Paul's speeches or uses a firsthand account.

As in Greek historians, the speeches in Acts often occur at important points in the action or in unusual and interesting situations. Greek historians also use speeches as ways of dramatically setting forth conflicting policies in debate, as Luke does in Acts 15, and Thucydides, followed to some extent by the Roman historians Sallust, Livy, and Tacitus, uses them as ways of indicating how events may be interpreted. They bring out the issues in the narrative. Certainly many of the major themes of Acts are most evident in the speeches. The speeches also show the apostles, Peter and Paul in particular, performing their duty of preaching the gospel, both to Jews and to gentiles. As such, the missionary sermons in Acts need not be exactly what was said on the specific occasion identified, but they remain valuable examples of the type of preaching practiced in synagogues and elsewhere. Peter or Paul often doubtless repeated the same message before different audiences, but to show them doing so is unnecessary in a literary work. In addition, the speeches in Acts are often too short for the occasions to which they are attributed, being perhaps summaries of what might have been said. Luke has exercised considerable restraint in literary elaboration of his speeches; those in the classical historians are generally much longer.

Luke is a reasonably skilled writer of speeches. He sometimes fails to tell us things we would like to know, and the speeches rarely achieve the eloquence of John's Gospel or of passages in Paul's epistles, but the arguments are mostly well suited to a particular audience, occasion, and speaker. Ideas recur, but are expressed in different ways, for different purposes. Although he does not attempt to reproduce the personal diction or mannerisms of the speakers (classical historians do not do so, either), Peter, Stephen, Gamaliel, the town clerk of Ephesus, and Agrippa come across as distinct personalities. A few remarks on Paul's speeches in Acts are reserved for the end of this chapter.

The following discussion consists of notes on some rhetorical features of discourses in Acts consisting of four or more verses. More could be said about most speeches. Some comments on the historicity of individual speeches are included, since this is a matter of special interest to some readers. The selections are discussed in the order of their occurrence in the text; here and there remarks on other rhetorically interesting passages appear as unnumbered sections in the sequence.

1. Speech of Peter, 1:16–22. Verses 18–19 are editorializing by Luke. The situation is the first meeting of the eleven disciples in Jerusalem after the ascension, and the exigence is Peter's perception of a need to fill the vacancy among the disciples caused by the defection and death of Judas. Peter bases this need on Scripture: "His office let another take" (1:20). He regards the disciples as the official witnesses of the resurrection and apparently feels there must be a full complement of such witnesses. He assumes leadership in the group without opposition and faces no great rhetorical problem. The speech thus requires little amplification. The proem is the single word "brethren" (1:16), often used with a friendly audience. There is then a brief narration, Luke's inserted description of Judas' death, the proof that action should be taken, based on Scripture, and the conclusion drawn from the situation and the text. Because the speech recommends an action in the (near) future, it is deliberative. To a classicist it is somewhat reminiscent of short speeches in the *Iliad* in which one of the heroes briefly describes the situation and ends with a recommendation for action, a very natural form of rhetoric. There is nothing unexpected in the contents of the speech. Given the knowledge that it was Peter who took the leadership role among the disciples and given a desire to dramatize an important event by prosopopoeia, Luke has created a predictable result.

2. Speech of Peter, 2:14–36, 38–39, 40b. The situation is the descent of the Holy Spirit manifested by speaking in tongues. The exigence is the bewilderment of the crowd and Peter's desire that they should correctly understand what is happening. Luke inserts a speech to dramatize and interpret the event. Peter is again shown assuming leadership; the audience is friendly, and there is no serious rhetorical problem provided he can get their attention. His initial address to them is formal and polite: "Men of Judea." The great interest of this speech is that it is the first example of a type of Christian preaching in which a speaker seizes upon some occasion, situation, or sign and uses it as a way to lead into the proclamation of the gospel. The result is sometimes the combination of two species of rhetoric. Here, verses 14–36 are judicial and are divided into two parts: verses 14–21, which are a refutation of the charge that those speaking in tongues are drunk, and verses 22–36, which are an indictment of the Jews for killing Jesus. The rhetorical function of the indictment is to amplify by contrast the innocence of those on whom the Holy Spirit has descended. The stasis in both cases is one of fact. After an interruption, the speech continues in a deliberative form (2:38–39, 40b). Verse 40a indicates that the speech was considerably longer than that presented here, or more accurately, that Luke thought a longer speech would have been given.

If we view the speech as a whole we see that it begins with a proem (14b), more extended than that of Peter's first speech because of his need to get the attention of a noisy crowd. This is followed by a proposition in the form of an enthymeme (2:15) and a scriptural explanation of what is happening, taken from Joel 2:28–32. Then comes a second proem (2:22) and the indictment of the Jews (23), where the argument is first supported from Scripture (25–28), then amplified by an exegesis of the passage, and then supported by another scriptural quotation, with a conclusion (36).

The success of Peter's speech is seen in the question from his audience: "Brethren, what shall we do?" Peter answers this question with a proposition in 2:38–39, which is an exhortation to action: "Repent and be baptized." This converts the speech into deliberative rhetoric. Scriptural authority is assumed to have been cited and referred to in verse 40. The

second half of that verse is the epilogue. Luke represents the
speech as entirely successful (2:41–42). In terms of the circumstances, this can be attributed to the miraculous sign of speaking in tongues; in terms of the rhetoric, to Peter's adroit utilization of the sign.

In composing this speech, all Luke need have known was
the incident which prompted it. Clearly someone had to speak,
and Peter was the most likely candidate; that he actually had
spoken may of course have been remembered. Although the
speech is more striking than that in chapter 1, the topics of
which it is composed are ones which Luke clearly regarded as
typical of the rhetoric of leaders of the early Church: the accusation that the Jews had killed Jesus and the seizing of an
occasion to proclaim the gospel. The amplification comes
from the scriptural evidence which is cited and which was as
available to Luke as to Peter.

3. Speech of Peter, 3:12–26. Both Luke's technique of composition and the rhetorical strategy attributed to Peter are essentially the same here as in the speech just examined. Peter has
cured a lame man at the gate of the temple, and the sight of the
man walking and leaping and praising God attracts a great deal
of public attention, which Peter seeks to use to preach the
gospel. The first section (2:12–18) is judicial and seeks to explain what has happened, attributing it to God, and by contrast indicting the Jews for the death of Jesus. As in the previous speech, the contrast (curing/killing) amplifies Peter's
action. The initial stasis is metastasis, transference of the responsibility for what he has done, a form of stasis of quality.
The question whether such healing was within the law does
not seem to be raised here, but Peter certainly does not admit
to any crime. He denies his own authority, but claims the
authority of God. The intellectual complexity of Paul's discussions of authority are lacking, and Luke portrays Peter as simple and direct.

The judicial section functions as proem and narration for
the deliberative speech, which is here given in fuller form than

in the speech in chapter 2 (no. 2 above). This is followed by the proposition (19–21), proof based on Scripture (22-25), and epilogue (26). The speech is presented as successful with many (4:4), though it awakened the hostility of the priests and Sadducees.

Hostility to the gospel supplies Acts throughout with a dramatic "plot," which here moves toward a climax in the death of Stephen and then in the second half (assuming it is the work of the same author) rises to a second climax in the trial of Paul. Dissension among Christians on the observance of the law provides a subplot for the first half of Acts, represented as happily resolved by the compromise of James (no. 13 below).

4. *Speech of Peter, 4:8–12.* Peter and the other disciples have been arrested and brought before the high priest, the elders, and the scribes. The exigence is the demand "By what power or by what name did you do this?" (4:7). The situation is clearly judicial, and the audience is hostile to a greater degree than in the previous speech. The implication is that Peter is acting with some infernal, magical power. He replies, "full with the Holy Spirit": these words are not his, but are given to him by God. The speech is a very short version of what Peter has said in two previous speeches, but with two distinctive features: he immediately labels his action a "good deed" (verse 9), thus establishing the stasis as one of quality; and the deliberative section is only implied by the words in verse 12, which take the form of an enthymeme. The reaction of the audience is to remark at Peter's boldness (that is, his confident tone of proclamation) and lack of education, which may refer to the relative absence of documentation, limited to one reference to the Psalms in verse 11. The speech is thus a radical response relying almost entirely on ethos, making no effort to conciliate the hostile audience, and as it were daring them to act. Peter and John are warned not to repeat the action, but insist they must speak what they have seen and heard, and the Council is afraid to take any action because of popular support for Peter.

5. *The Apostles' Prayer, 4:24–30.* A prayer can be epideictic (as is a prayer of thanksgiving), judicial (as is a prayer for forgiveness), or deliberative (as is a prayer for help). This is a deliberative prayer, as verses 29–30 make clear, for the speakers request continuation of the powers of inspired speech and miracle-working which have been manifested by Peter. Verses 24b–26 are a proem, with amplification of the greatness of God. This amplification is itself epideictic, in that it strengthens the belief of the speakers of the prayer and of those who hear them. In primitive society such amplification was probably originally regarded as persuasive with the divinity addressed: the gods liked to be flattered. Verses 27–28 are a narration, which also strengthens belief by noting the victory that has been achieved over Jesus' enemies. Verses 29–30 are the actual supplication, which is placed here in a structure resembling that of a simple deliberative speech such as that in chapter 1 (no. 1 above). The prayer is probably a traditional one, quoted verbatim by Luke.

6. *Speech of Peter and the Apostles before the Council, 5:29–32.* This judicial speech resembles that at 4:8–12 (no. 4), with two differences. The charge this time is not the healing of a cripple by some suspect power, but violation of the injunction of the priests. This cannot be justified as a "good deed," and the stasis is thus metastasis, transference of responsibility to God (29b). The other difference is the citation of witnesses as proof in verse 32. What we find in the text is really just an outline of the topics of a speech such as would have been given on the occasion.

7. *Speech of Gamaliel to the Council, 5:35–39.* The question before the Council is what to do about the insubordination of the apostles. Gamaliel, as a learned Pharisee, speaks with external authority. His proem (35b) warns of the seriousness of the situation. He then cites precedents, as a teacher of the law might be expected to do, from which he draws an inductive conclusion: "Keep away from these men and let them alone."

This he supports with a disjunctive hypothetical enthymeme: "For if this plan or this undertaking is of men, it will fail; but if it is of God, you will not be able to overthrow them" (38–39). As read by Luke's Christian audience the statement has great meaning, but it is a perfectly sound piece of advice which a judicious man might have said. In these verses Luke has well captured the mode of thought of a teacher of the law, and it is possible that it is attributed to Gamaliel as a well-known legal scholar rather than on historical evidence that he spoke at this time. A legal scholar doubtless would have cited a precedent, though not necessarily this particular one. In structure the speech resembles the simple deliberative plan seen in 1:16–22 (no. 1) and elsewhere, but the examples replace the narrative otherwise found.

8. *Speech of Stephen before the Council, 7:2–53.* The situation is a trial for blasphemy, specifically that Stephen has said that Jesus will destroy the temple and change the customs of Moses; hostile witnesses are furnished (6:13–14). The exigence is provided by the words of the high priest, "Is this so?" (7:1). The rhetorical problem is acute: Stephen clearly concludes that there is no real possibility of making the Council understand the message of Jesus, he expresses anger at his persecutors, and he deliberately invites martyrdom. The words "full of the Holy Spirit" (7:55), applied to Stephen at the end of the speech, are probably to be extended to the whole of his remarks. He speaks throughout the words that are given to him. The stasis can be viewed as *antengklema*, counteraccusation, but the effect of that, as often, is to imply a rejection of the right of the tribunal to try him, which is stasis of jurisdiction. Stephen's hostility to the Council is only gradually revealed. His proem (7:2a) uses the word "brethren," which Peter has used to friendly audiences, and the narration, which constitutes the bulk of the speech (2b–48), at first seems objective, but an element of indictment is gradually introduced (for example, at 25 and 39). This leads to a proposition (51) attacking the Jews in general, which is briefly supported by historical evidence

(52–53). Rhetorically the speech is incomplete: it needs either a return to the charge against Stephen, with an explicit rejection of the right of the Council to try him, or a deliberative epilogue calling for repentence, as in the speeches of Peter. An epilogue is, however, supplied to the rhetorical unit of the story of Stephen by the vision of 54–56, which constitutes proof of the rightness of Stephen's cause both for himself and for the readers of Acts. As a result of this transcendent vision, Stephen can acquit his persecutors: "Lord, do not hold this sin against them" (60). God, not the Council, is the real judge.

Although it is unlikely that the speech was written down at the time, and Luke's text cannot be accepted as a word-for-word account of what Stephen said, there are factors in the situation which point to a degree of historicity in our version. The first martyrdom was a turning point for the Church, and the substance of what Stephen said may thus have been remembered. Although the speech uses common topics, it is unusual in tone and in its incomplete structure. Finally, the attribution to the Holy Spirit gives it some of the qualities of sacred language and thus attracts special veneration. Against this, however, it should be noted that Luke probably felt that the Holy Spirit was speaking through himself throughout his own composition, making him inclined to rely on his intuition.

9. *Speech of Peter, 10:34–43.* This is the first pure example of kerygmatic preaching. Though the gospel is proclaimed in earlier speeches, it has been coupled with indictment of the Jews. The situation here is created by the invitation of the gentile centurion Cornelius that Peter tell "all you have been commanded by the Lord" (10:33). Peter has external authority from the vision sent to Cornelius, and he has no serious rhetorical problem. His proem (34–35) lacks any word of direct address, but graciously acknowledges the extension of the gospel to the gentiles. This is a situation into which the apostles have been pushed by Jewish hostility, but which has been validated for them by external signs. The narration (36–42) reviews the

prophecy of John, the anointment of Jesus, the crucifixion, the resurrection, and the commandment to preach the gospel and to testify that Jesus has been ordained to be judge of the living and the dead. This could be taken in personal terms; nothing is said about the early end of the age. Demonstration of the truth of the message is by direct evidence, including the miracles of Jesus and the witness of the apostles. The only enthymeme occurs in verse 38: "for God was with him." There is little amplification except in verse 41, where a second relative clause adds emphasis to the witness of the apostles, "who ate and drank with him after he rose from the dead." The actual situation would seem to have required a more extensive address than is given here. Peter would probably have given an account of his dream and of the circumstances which brought him to this occasion, but this is unnecessary in the economy of Luke's literary account. His compositional hand is thus clearly at work. The speech itself is epideictic, focusing on belief; the decision to baptize gentiles is a reaction to the pouring forth of the Holy Spirit after the speech rather than to any appeal initiated by Peter such as that in 2:38.

10. Speech of Peter, 11:4–18. This is Peter's defense before the circumcision party, which accuses him of violating the law in associating with gentiles. He admits the fact and the contravention of the law but assigns responsibility to God, thus employing metastasis. The audience, though critical of his action, is Christian and willing to entertain Peter's basic argument, that the order of God takes precedence over the law. The format is a personal narration "in order" (11:4), that is, "from beginning to end." No proem is supplied, but Peter probably would have said "brethren." The tone is very personal and the speech persuasive because of Peter's external authority and his ability to project an internal ethos, chiefly a matter of candor: he had protested to God at being told to violate the law (8). No evidence is given other than Peter's own words, and the only argumentation comes at the end: "If then God gave the same gift to them as he gave to us when we believed in the

Lord Jesus Christ, who was I that I could withstand God?"
The rhetorical question has a pathetic appeal: "What would
you have done?" The speech is presented by Luke as entirely
successful (18).

In Acts 12:21 Herod (Agrippa I), dressed in his royal robes and
seated on his throne (that is, with all the trappings of external
authority), gives a formal address to the people. It is no part of
Luke's purpose to reveal its contents. Herod is proclaimed a
god by the people—and falls dead. Josephus gives a somewhat
different account (*Jewish Antiquities* 19.343–52), in which the
popular salutation to the king is followed by a heart attack.
Herod, knowing that he is dying, then gives a brief, pathetic
address. The two accounts show how difficult it is to know
whether details in Acts are exact and how much they may have
been rearranged on the basis of the values and message of the
writer. Josephus too had causes to plead.

11. Speech of Paul, 13:16–41. Paul has set out on his first missionary journey, preaching in synagogues. The first speech reported is delivered in Antioch in Pisidia on a sabbath after the
regular Jewish service, with reading of the law and the prophets. The rulers of the synagogue then invite Paul to speak, "if
you have any word of exhortation for the people" (13:15). Paul
stands and motions with his hand. In 12:17 Peter is described
as using a gesture of the hand to secure silence, and that is
probably the case here, despite the temptation to associate
Paul's behavior with the words at 13:17: "and with uplifted
arm he led them out of it." Reference to the gesture might
suggest that Luke was present and remembered it, but something like it is mentioned again (21:40) and was doubtless
usual when a preacher sought to begin his remarks. Despite
the call for an exhortation, which implies a deliberative speech,
Paul's remarks are epideictic, aiming at belief, not at action.
The rhetorical problem is chiefly Jewish hostility to Jesus, but
since the Pisidian Jews bear no responsibility for that hostility,
Paul avoids any indictment of them and seeks to explain why

hostility existed in Jerusalem (27). Paul does not know his audience, and his brief proem is rather formal (16b). The narration (17–25) is a survey of events from the Egyptian captivity to John the Baptist. These would be familiar to the audience and help to establish Paul's basis of communication with them. Then comes a proposition, "to us has been sent the message of this salvation" (26), and a proof (27–37), explaining the circumstances of Jesus' death, which is attributed to the ignorance, not the wickedness, of Jews, and claiming witness of his resurrection, with citation of scriptural prophecy. An epilogue (38–39) summarizes the message and warns against disregarding the prophecy. This is an element of pathos. As usual in Acts, the early end of the age is not mentioned. The speech can probably be taken as a typical example of the contents of Paul's preaching under similar conditions.

Paul is successful in interesting the congregation and is asked to speak again on the next sabbath. This time a large crowd of Jews and gentiles collects, some of the Jews revealing hostility. Paul and Barnabas spurn the Jewish opposition; the gospel must be proclaimed; since the Jews reject it, they will preach to the gentiles (46–47).

12. Speech of Peter, 15:7–11. The apostles and elders are deliberating whether circumcision and other observances of Jewish law are to be required of new converts. There was "much debate" (15:7), of which the speeches of Peter and James are briefly reported as well as the letter sent to Antioch to resolve the question. Luke deliberately avoids dramatizing the radical Jewish viewpoint. Peter's speech takes up his remarks in chapter 11 (no. 10 above). He appears to be trying to get others to identify with his extension of the gospel to the gentiles, the validity of which he claims they all know (15:7). This is not strictly relevant to the question at issue. On that matter he advances only one argument: that to demand strict obedience to the law would "make trial of God by putting a yoke upon the neck of the disciples which neither our fathers nor we have been able to bear" (10). As in his previous speech, this argument is cast as a rhetorical question. Two points are implied in this argument: first, that the Jews themselves have had difficulty living up to the law and that it is thus unrealistic to expect others to accept it; second, that to demand obedience to the law by those not born into the Jewish tradition will make it much harder for some to accept the gospel, and thus will "try God." This may be assumed to apply particularly to circumcision, which for an adult (without anaesthesia or sedatives during several weeks of recovery) is notoriously painful and sometimes the effective equivalent of sexual mutilation. God would have to instill great resolution in the hearts of converts to persuade them to undergo the rite. Both of Peter's arguments are somewhat pragmatic, as suits his character, and much simpler than the theological arguments advanced by Paul in his epistles. It is not clear whether these issues, which could be viewed as a conflict between principle and expediency, were directly faced in the debate or only alluded to indirectly as they are by Peter here.

13. *The Compromise of James, 15:12–21.* Paul and Barnabas side with Peter, reporting signs and wonders done among the gentiles. It is God's will, therefore, that the gospel be extended. James uses the evidence of Peter and Old Testament prophecy to establish the point that the gospel should be extended and proposes a compromise under which only four requirements of the law, not including circumcision, should be retained. Verse 21 ostensibly gives his reason, but in fact it is not a reason why these four requirements are the essential ones, nor does that appear from the prophecy cited (16–18). Luke seems to have overlooked a necessary part of James' speech or to have omitted a reference to previous discussion of these four laws. The argument would have been that they were pre-Mosaic and applied to all mankind, not just to the children of Israel. His account of the debate is not very satisfactory; that may result from unsatisfactory sources, from unstated assumptions, or from a desire to mute the dissension. He certainly moves to

end this part of his account on a very positive note of Christian unity.

The letter of Acts 15:23–29 resembles the rescript of a Roman magistrate responding to a query from a subordinate and has the rhetorical characteristics of a public letter of the Roman period. That could mean that it is genuine, but it unfortunately also means that it is exactly the kind of letter which Luke could have composed with limited knowledge of the contents. The letter well expresses the ethos of the senders and their concern for their brethren at Antioch, but again no explanation is given of the logical basis of the decision.

Acts 1:1–15:35 seems to be a compositional unit and could be read as a complete work. The disciples have carried on the mission of Jesus and seem to have settled their internal differences; faced with Jewish opposition they have persevered, and the gospel is being extended to the gentiles. From 15:36 to the end of the book, focus is turned entirely upon the missionary activities of Paul; Peter and the other apostles are forgotten. Beginning in 16:10 the first person plural is occasionally used in the narrative, creating a tone of personal witness. It is generally assumed that Luke joined Paul at this point and is here giving his own account of events, but it is odd that he does not specifically mention this, and Timothy, rather than Luke, is introduced as Paul's new associate. Again in chapter 20 Timothy joins Paul and the narrative slips into the first person plural. ("These" in 20:5 need refer only to Tychicus and Trophimus.) It is possible that Luke utilized Timothy's account of his travels with Paul and did not alter "we" to "they." This is unlikely to be an editorial oversight, considering the number of times it occurs and the otherwise smooth flow of the narrative. Except for the use of "we" there is no significant change in style, and the compositional methods of the next two speeches are similar to those employed in the first half of Acts. Apparently "we" did not hear either of these speeches; Timothy clearly did not. Firsthand knowledge of what Paul said begins in chapter 20, when Timothy is present, and the speech there is rather different from what has gone before.

Acts 1:1–15:35 may represent a compositional unit which was all that was originally intended to be added to Luke's Gospel. Classical historiography generally does not employ a rhetorical epilogue and instead often concludes with a very brief reference to continuing events (as at the end of Acts 28). This well describes where we are left in Acts 15:30–35. The opening of 15:36 is reminiscent of the opening of Xenophon's *Hellenica*, a work read in Greek schools. Xenophon attached his work on Greek history to the abrupt end of Thucydides (probably as left at the latter's death) by the words *meta de tauta*, "And after this . . . ." Acts 15:36 begins "And after some days . . . ." An educated audience such as Luke had in mind might have perceived this.

If in fact the second half of Acts is Luke's version of Paul's travels, conceived as a separate entity and based on Timothy's account filled out by Luke for those periods Timothy did not witness, the retention of the "we" is not an editorial oversight, but a stylistic rhetorical device to increase the authority of the account. No deceit need have been intended; Luke may have thought that the introduction of Timothy in chapter 16 made clear what he was doing, and it is possible that 15:36 was intended to be given a title such as "Luke's Account of the Missions of Paul, after Timothy." The result would have been a loosely connected corpus in three parts: the Gospel, the activities of the disciples from the ascension to the meeting in Jerusalem, and the missions of Paul. In the third part, although there is little difference in the prose, there is considerable difference in tone resulting from firsthand observation and from a movement beyond Palestine, Syria, and Pisidia to the Ionian coast, Greece, and beyond. In this new setting Paul's speech at Athens, the first address in what might be called Second Acts, takes on special meaning. Not only the Jews reject the gospel; so do the philosophers of the intellectual capital of the world. There is a dramatic movement from rejection in Athens, to rejection in Jerusalem and Paul's trial, to rejection in Rome, but this rejection by leaders everywhere is shown against a pattern of acceptance by the people.

In the second part of Acts Paul preaches in synagogues and occasionally elsewhere. Some of his discourses were extensive; in Thessalonica, for example, he argued with the Jews in synagogues for three weeks (17:2). Other evidence of long single speeches will be cited below.

14. Paul's Areopagus Speech, 17:22–31. The rhetorical situation of this celebrated speech is described in some detail. Paul is in Athens, waiting for Silas and Timothy (who thus did not hear the speech) and is offended at the many idols in the city (17:16). His distress, even anger, establishes a basically judicial situation, though of course his ultimate goal is a deliberative one, to convince any audience to embrace Christianity. He argues in the synagogue with Jews and in the agora with anyone who will listen to him and succeeds in arousing a somewhat hostile interest on the part of certain Stoics and Epicureans. Athens in the Roman period was a "university town," the seat of the philosophical schools. This is referred to contemptuously in verse 21. Paul's interlocutors are perhaps not the heads of these schools, but their contentious students. They must have been largely Stoics; Paul's arguments are cast in terms which would be comprehensible to Stoics, not Epicureans, and Epicureanism was not very strong in this period. Cynics and Academics may well have been in the audience as well. They label him a babbler and accuse him of preaching foreign divinities. Finally they take him to the Areopagus and demand that he justify his teachings. The passage has usually been taken to refer to the hill of the Areopagus, but more likely the setting of the speech was the Royal Stoa at the northwest corner of the agora, where the Council of the Areopagus met in this period. "Areopagus" thus means the court of the Areopagus, which had jurisdiction over religious offenses. We know from the sequel (17:34) that at least one member of the court was present, and probably there was a quorum. It seems therefore that the author of Acts intends us to view the occasion as a preliminary legal hearing which might lead to a formal indictment. The result is a continuation of the case: "We will hear you again about this" (17:32). The matter seems to have ended with Paul's withdrawal from Athens.

Paul addresses this court with the conventional form found in the Greek orators as an address to heliastic courts, "Men of Athens." Luke may not have realized that this was not appropriate for the Areopagus, where the address would probably simply have been "Gentlemen," but the longer phrase well suits the function of the speech as outlined above. There is no further attempt at a proem and no attempt to establish Paul's personal authority. The fact is, he had none. The body of the speech falls into two parts: 22b–28 is a refutation of the charge that he is teaching a foreign divinity; 29–31 is a prosecution of the religious errors of the Athenians and ends by preaching the gospel. In the defense Paul uses the altar of the unknown god as a sign that the god he preaches is not foreign. He then describes this god in terms that would be comprehensible to Stoics. What Paul means by saying that God made the world and what Stoics would understand by that are rather different, but Stoics could easily accept the enthymeme that God does not live in shrines and is not served by human hands, since he needs nothing from man and in fact gives man life and breath (25). Paul's usual techniques of proof are adapted to a Greek audience. He makes no use of Jewish history, which would have been scorned or accounted meaningless, and he cites as external evidence not the Scriptures, but Greek poets (28). From this picture of the nature of God, Paul draws the conclusion that God ought not to be thought of as a representation of the art and imagination of men. This seems a logical *non sequitur* in our highly compressed text, because the unknown God is worshiped without an image; but the conclusion helps to convert defense into attack. Philosophical Greeks usually acquiesced in pagan worship of idols, even though they did not believe the idol was literally a god.

Now that he is on the offensive, Paul calls his audience ignorant and demands their repentance, introducing pathos by confidently predicting the end of the world. This is one of the very few specific references to that doctrine in Acts, but in itself it would not have astonished a Greek audience. Stoics believed that the world would be destroyed and also that God or his agents judged the dead, though they usually did not associate the two events because they viewed the destruction as part of a natural cycle, rather than as a judgment in itself. At the very end Paul introduces the only specifically Christian doctrine, the resurrection of Christ. For this he supplies no evidence, and the remark leads some to mock him. The concept is not necessarily impossible for a Stoic (Heracles was a stoic hero who had descended into the underworld and returned), but the assertion would seem to require some evidence if the speech was to succeed. Paul might have cited witnesses, perhaps even described his experience on the Damascus road. Certainly he would have done so in his discourses in the synagogues. The abrupt end of the speech as we have it seems to be part of the rhetoric of the author of Acts, who throughout the passage seeks to polarize the situation. He clearly holds the philosophers in some contempt and wishes to leave a picture of Paul as the radical Christian amid the mocking and ignorant philosophers. But if Paul actually delivered a speech like this, he made a remarkable effort to carry the gospel to the gentiles in terms they might have understood. He had only limited success and left Athens, abruptly it seems, for Corinth, which was at the time the capital of the Roman province of Greece. There he stayed a year and a half. When brought before Gallio, the governor (and brother of the great Stoic philosopher Seneca), on the complaint of local Jews, the case against him was summarily dismissed by Gallio as a matter outside his responsibility.

As 1 and 2 Corinthians demonstrate, some Corinthians found Paul lacking in philosophy and eloquence. Apollos was more successful in this respect. He is first met in Acts 18:24, where he is described as both eloquent and well-versed in Scripture. He "powerfully confuted the Jews in public, showing by the Scriptures that the Christ was Jesus." In method this is not unlike the preaching of Paul, but it must have differed considerably in style. It is a pity that the author of Acts did not attempt an example of Apollos' preaching, but that would have detracted from his portrait of Paul.

15. Speech of the Town Clerk of Ephesus, 19:35–40. Paul's ministry to Ephesus, viewed locally as an economic threat to the livelihood of the artisans of pagan idols, has resulted in a riot. The *grammateus*, or clerk of the town council, delivers a realistic deliberative speech to calm the crowd. He relies heavily on his ethos. In his proem (19:35) he treats the question of the greatness of Ephesus' pagan shrines as beyond debate. His proposition, like that of Gamaliel (no. 7 above), is that the crowd should do nothing rash. His argument (37–39) is that Paul and his friends have done nothing sacrilegious and that the lawcourts are open if there are complaints from individuals. His epilogue (40) appeals to civic pride. Timothy did not hear this speech, and it was probably composed on the basis of what was likely to have been said.

Paul's addresses were almost certainly longer than what is usually attributed to him in Acts. Speaking to the Christians of Troas when they met to break bread on the first day of the week (thus in the morning), he prolonged his discourse until midnight (20:7). What he said in such an extended discourse is unknown, but can perhaps be imagined as a combination of exegesis of prophecy, exposition of the gospel, and theological disquisition, with refutation of other views as seen in the epistles, the whole interspersed with personal experiences, scriptural quotations, prayers, and exhortations. Such a sermon would be more repetitive than the epistles and more discursive or less carefully structured.

16. Paul's Farewell Address at Miletus to the Elders of Ephesus, 20:18–35. As noted in Chapter 3, the farewell address is a Greek epideictic form, but Paul's discourse here does not accord with the rhetorical conventions described by Menander Rhetor. On first reading, it may appear to look to the past and to be a defense of Paul's actions, with some advice for the future, but careful consideration reveals that the apostle's major concern throughout is with the future, including how his past ministry will be considered in the future. The function of the first half (20:18–27) is therefore not to defend Paul's ministry, but to establish his ethos in the eyes of the Ephesians and himself, and it may be viewed as an extended proem. Even within this section the most important topic is probably the anticipation of martyrdom seen in verses 23–24. A strong note of pathos is here combined with ethos. With that basis for appeal laid down, Paul then states a proposition in verse 28: "Take heed to yourselves and to all the flock, in which the Holy Spirit has made you overseers, to care for the church of God, which he obtained with the blood of his Son." The two relative clauses support the proposition and have the effect of an enthymeme. Paul then prophesies about the future as the Ephesians will see it, employing the metaphor of the wolf coming on the flock (29). His own past sufferings will be an example for them (31). The poignant epilogue (32–35) commends the Ephesians to God, resumes the topic of Paul's ministry, and identifies the Ephesians with Paul, reinforcing this with a quotation from Jesus. The speech had a moving effect on the Ephesians, and it is indeed the most personal of the apostle's discourses in Acts, and the finest. It is also the first speech in Acts which "we" heard personally, as indicated by the repeated use of the first person in the chapter, and thus could be quite close to what was actually said. That this is so is further confirmed by similarities of style and content to Paul's writing in the epistles, especially in the Epistle to the Philippians. Philippians is one of the last letters, written in Rome shortly after the events described in Acts and thus possibly close to the time that Timothy may have written up an account of his travels with Paul. If Timothy became bishop of Ephesus, as has often been believed, he would have had a special interest in the apostle's farewell to his own church.

17. Speech of the Brethren to Paul in Jerusalem, 21:20–25. On arrival in Jerusalem, Paul was warmly but apprehensively greeted by the Christian community and advice was given to him by several of its leaders, here cast in the form of a single speech which the narrator personally heard (21:18). Greek historians (see, for example, Thucydides 1.68) occasionally use this technique of attributing a speech to more than one spokesman to indicate a community decision or to sum up in compressed form what several speakers said. This speech follows the simple deliberative pattern we observed in the early speeches in Acts. A proem sets forth the need for action (20–22). This is followed by specific advice, supported by a reason (23–24).

18. Paul's Speech to the Jews of Jerusalem, 22:3–22. The effort to conciliate the Jews, described in chapter 21, failed. To prevent a riot Paul was put into protective custody by a Roman tribune, but he persuaded the officer to allow him to make an appeal to the crowd with the soldiers as personal protection. The speech is judicial and entirely a narration of Paul's former activities against the Christians and his subsequent conversion and commission to the gentiles. It was delivered in Hebrew (22:2) as an ethical device to show Paul's own Jewishness. This is the only place where the language of a speech is identified. The speeches of Peter and others in the first half of Acts were probably in Aramaic. On his missionary journeys, when speaking in synagogues Paul may sometimes have used Aramaic, but if gentiles were present he probably spoke in Greek, and he may have used Greek exclusively in Corinth. Paul begins with a gesture (21:40), here probably the palm of his right hand with fingers extended as a request for silence from the crowd. His reference to his education with Gamaliel in the "strict manner of the law of our fathers" (22:3) is also of course an ethical appeal to the crowd. Since Paul does not deny that his actions have been inconsistent with the law, the stasis is best regarded as metastasis, transferring responsibility for his actions to God. Paul is interrupted by the crowd at the first reference to the gentiles. If he had been allowed to continue he would presumably have cited evidence from Scripture, and if the Holy Spirit had warmed the hearts of the crowd he might even have hoped to conclude with an exhortation to repent and be saved. That proved impossible.

In chapter 23, brought before the Council, Paul gives no formal speech but is examined as in a legal hearing and employs a diversionary tactic. Something rather like this is occasionally seen in Greek oratory, as when Aeschines, speaking at Delphi, turned the attention of the Amphictionic Council from the issue at hand to the illegal occupation of sacred land by the Amphissians (*Against Ctesiphon* 107). Here Paul perceives that his audience is part Sadducee, part Pharisee, and makes an *ad hominem* appeal to the Pharisees by a diversionary reference to the resurrection of the dead. The Pharisees as a result take up his cause, while Paul himself is escorted out by the tribune and sent to the governor of Syria with a letter indicating that he is a Roman citizen who has broken no civil law. His accusers are ordered to make their complaints to the governor. The tactics attributed to Paul on both of these occasions may well be those he actually employed; "we" are not mentioned, but were probably present.

19. Speech of Tertullus to Felix, 24:2–8. The high priest Ananias and the elders follow through the prosecution and are represented before the governor Felix by the "rhetor" Tertullus. He is apparently a professional patron at the bar, familiar with the procedure and language of Roman courts. His name is Latin and he may have addressed Felix in that language, probably at greater length than in the speech given here. In a conventional classical proem he flatters the governor (24:2–4), alleges that Paul is a Nazarene agitator who has profaned the temple, and asks the governor to interrogate him. The Jews subscribe to the charges and offer themselves as witnesses to prove it (9).

20. Paul's Defense before Felix, 24:10–21. The speech is judicial, the stasis fact: Paul denies that he has engaged in disputation or stirred up a crowd (12) or that he has profaned the temple (18). He begins with a short and respectful proem, couched in a good classical Greek periodic sentence (10), which he follows with an equally short narration (11) and proposition (12). Some use is made of Greek proverbs (14, 26). The rest of the speech is devoted to proof, with no epilogue. Paul admits belonging to "the way" (14), which was not known to be illegal, and claims that he had purified himself before entering the temple (18), that the accusation is not being made by those who witnessed the incident (19), and that it is not specific (20), but he admits that he did speak of the resurrection of the dead. He refrains from pointing out that this doctrine was supported by the Pharisees. That may be an omission by the author of Acts on the ground that the point had been made before in his narrative (23:6–9), though possibly it would not have been a useful point with the governor. Since he presents no evidence to support what he says, Paul must be regarded as relying on ethos—chiefly his confident candor—and on the legal assumption that he is innocent unless his prosecutors can document his guilt. The disinclination of Roman officials to enforce Jewish religious law is of course strongly in his favor, but that is left unvoiced.

Felix continues the case pending the arrival of the tribune who had arrested Paul, a necessary witness. He holds Paul in custody but allows him visitors, presumably including the narrator, and invites him to speak before himself and his Jewish wife about Christianity. Apparently he finds public discussion unacceptable, either personally or because it tended to stir up feelings, and the conversations are conducted in private. This is said (24:27) to have gone on for two years, but that may mean that Felix served a total term of two years, in which case Paul's custody was much shorter. The delay was probably occasioned by the governor's wish to leave the decision to his successor, who had probably been named and was en route from Rome, but the narrator also says that Felix hoped to be bribed (24:26). When the new governor, Festus, arrives, the Jews renew their charges against Paul and Festus proposes a trial in Jerusalem. Paul refuses and appeals to Caesar. Festus accepts the appeal and orders him taken to Rome (25:12).

21 and 22. Addresses of Festus to Agrippa, 25:14–21 and 24–27. These two speeches are included because they fall within our criteria of four or more verses. They are chiefly of interest in revealing the point of view and legal interpretation of Festus, who gives a simple narrative of Paul's case. The object of the hearing is indicated in the final verse, to clarify the charges so that a written report can be sent to Rome. Within the rhetoric of Acts the speeches contribute a feeling of historicity.

23. Paul's Defense before Agrippa, 26:2–23. When compared to Paul's address to the Jews in Jerusalem and his defense before Felix (nos. 18 and 20 above), this speech shows an attempt to adapt the same basic materials to a different audience, in this case the hellenized Jewish king Agrippa. Paul has clearly had an opportunity to prepare his address in advance, something which was not possible when he spoke in Jerusalem. Stasis remains metastasis, transference of responsibility to God. The rhetorical question of verse 8 is reminiscent of the device used by Peter in addressing the Christians of Jerusalem. There are elegances of style which Agrippa would have appreciated, for example the litotes of verse 19.

The graceful proem (2–3) is intended both for Agrippa and for Festus, since it embraces Festus' purpose in getting the advice of Agrippa on a subject he is well suited to judge. There follows a narration in which Paul omits reference to Gamaliel and to his own blindness, but adds the fact that God had addressed him in Hebrew. The report of the direct address functions as an authoritative witness. The proof (19–23) argues that Paul (like Peter) had no choice and adds scriptural evidence. But when Paul refers to preaching to the gentiles he is again interrupted, this time, surprisingly, by Festus, who says,

"Paul, you are mad; your great learning is turning you mad" (24). "Too much reading" might be a better translation of *polla grammata*, as though Paul had been searching out prophecies. Paul protests that "these things" (the prophecies) are known to Agrippa and then resumes a more personal appeal to him (27).

The speech is partially successful in that Agrippa and Festus agree that Paul has done nothing wrong, but it is not so successful that they are willing to undertake any sponsorship of his cause or issue any rebuke to the priests. They would have set Paul free to take his chances if he had not appealed to Caesar (32), but as it is, to Rome he must go. Early Christians of course regarded this as part of God's plan; certainly it is difficult to see how, at this stage in the situation, a different rhetorical approach would have secured different results. Like Socrates, Paul regarded some kinds of rhetorical appeal as unacceptable: anything that departed from the truth as he understood it or from his duty to preach the gospel. Friendly witnesses to his conduct in Jerusalem existed and might have helped his case with Roman officials, but it may have been impractical for them to come forward, and most would not have had the stature before the court that the leaders of the Jewish community did. All of these factors pointed toward a tactic of relying upon ethos, supported where possible by scriptural prophecy. That ethos is an appealing one: the lonely figure of a human being who has had a transcendent religious experience and who seeks not to explain, but to express it in the most natural way possible.

24. Paul's Prophecy on Shipboard, 27:21–26. This appears to be primarily an epideictic, rather than deliberative speech, exhorting those on the ship to faith, with a prophecy that they will be saved, though the ship will be lost, on the basis of a dream Paul has had. The speech seems to have been included in Acts primarily because of this dream, in which an angel tells Paul not to fear, "you must stand before Caesar in Rome" (27:23). The incident is more reminiscent of experiences such as those of Aeneas in Virgil's *Aeneid* than of a truly oratorical situation. Nothing is said about the effect on the audience.

25. Paul's Address to the Jewish Leaders of Rome, 28:17–20. This is a short speech explaining why Paul has come to Rome, anticipating charges against him, and exonerating the Roman officials and the Jewish nation as a whole (28:19). He shows himself open to reconciliation. This speech can be regarded as a proem for subsequent preaching (even though that does not occur immediately), for its main objective is to establish an understanding with the local Jewish leaders. The ensuing discourse is not reported, but it extended from morning until evening (23) and resulted in some conversions (24). In verses 26–28 Paul expresses his frustration and his intention to turn to the gentiles instead, much as at Corinth (18:6).

Is the rhetoric of Paul in Acts the rhetoric of Paul in the epistles? Most readers would probably say no. The accounts in Acts lack his complicated dialectic, often projected in dialogue with himself, and do not show his fondness for pleonasm or for exploring the subtle meanings of words or new interpretations for old texts. Speeches attributed to Paul in Acts through chapter 19 do not appear to be based on a firsthand knowledge of what he actually said and have the characteristics of construction that Luke seems to have used in speeches attributed to Peter and others. The speech to the elders of Ephesus (20:18–35, no. 16 above) is the first in Acts that seems based on direct knowledge by the narrator, and the only speech really evocative of Paul's personal style, though simplified for use in an historiographic work. Subsequent speeches are not markedly Pauline in style, except perhaps the exchange with Agrippa. They seem to have been written with some knowledge of Paul's arguments, but probably not of his actual words. Yet it must be kept in mind that their audience is different from the audience addressed in the epistles; these are public addresses, for the most part, in which Paul's personal style would have been less appropriate and less effective. The epistles show that he could adapt his writing to his audience and the occasion: his tone with the Thessalonians is different from his tone with the Galatians, for example. It is very likely that his tone in Jerusalem was different from his tone in addressing the elders of Ephesus, and whatever was distinctive about it is further diluted by adaptation to a historical work and by the literary abilities of the writer or writers of Acts. The situation is slightly analogous to the portrayal of Socrates in Plato and Xenophon. Plato's Socrates is far more complicated and far more powerful. In Paul's epistles we have something more vivid than that: not the impression of an inspired pupil, but the actual words of the master.

Of the rhetorical features of Acts the most important historically is the way the apostles utilize occasions to preach the gospel. Whenever given an occasion to speak, even in defense of specific charges against them personally, they try to convert the situation into an opportunity to proclaim the message of Jesus and convert others. That is what really matters to them, not their personal danger, or the needs of the moment. This is generally true of Paul's epistles also and has remained a characteristic of Christian rhetoric.

Chapter Seven. Thessalonians, Galatians, Romans

The earliest of the epistles of Paul is apparently 1 Thessalonians, written from Corinth in the early 50s. The circumstances of Paul's visit to Thessalonica are briefly described in Acts 17. He had founded a small Christian community there, but awakened violent opposition from Jews and was forced to leave abruptly. The letter itself makes it clear (2:1–8) that the community is still hard pressed. In the absence of anyone with apostolic authority the Christians in Thessalonica are also internally troubled by doctrinal questions, which Paul attempts to answer in the latter part of the letter.

Most of Paul's epistles have two main parts. In the first, here chapters 1–3, he usually deals with the circumstances and general purpose of his letter; in the second, here chapters 4–5, he takes up specific questions. In the great theological epistles like 1 Corinthians, the first section provides the theological or doctrinal basis for the specific questions, and topics are enunciated which are then interwoven throughout the letter. We saw that this is also done in 2 Corinthians, and it can be found in a simpler way in 1 Thessalonians.

The structure of a Greco-Roman letter resembles a speech, framed by a salutation and complimentary closure. In the more elaborate letters, Romans for example, the salutation takes on rhetorical qualities and itself enunciates topics, a tradition continued by other early Christian writers like Ignatius of Antioch. In 1 Thessalonians the salutation is very simple; the only amplification is provided by the words "in God the Father and the Lord Jesus Christ" (1:1). The close is also a simple one, though it contains the important injunction that the letter should be read to the church (5:7).

First Thessalonians is basically deliberative, an exhortation to stand fast in the Lord (3:8) with specific advice for the Christian life, given in chapters 4–5. The presence of narrative in chapters 2–3 is not a sign of judicial rhetoric but rather, as we shall also see in Galatians, part of Paul's efforts to establish his ethos. Paul's rhetorical problem is the criticism of him being voiced in Thessalonica and his distance from the community; he seeks to meet this by identifying himself with the church and by stressing the continuity of their relationship. This desire is immediately clear in the first sentence of the letter: "We give thanks to God *always* for you, *constantly* mentioning you in our prayers" (1:2). The topic is taken up again toward the end of the narration: "praying earnestly night and day" (3:10).

The proem (1:2–10) seeks the goodwill of the audience, but it seeks more than that. Paul attempts to convert reciprocal goodwill into a basis of self-confidence on the part of the Thessalonians. The proem is therefore ethical, but supported by argumentation. He alludes to their faith, love, and hope as self-evident characteristics, topics to be reintroduced in 3:6, and reminds them that they have been chosen of God (1:4). This takes the form of an enthymeme, the proof of which is the presence of the Holy Spirit. Of this Paul himself, and his conduct in Thessalonica, is a witness, and the Thessalonians have become an imitator of him and of God and a model for all others (1:7). The evidence for that in turn is their reputation beyond Macedonia, of which Paul is again witness. Paul may have wanted to believe this, but it is doubtful whether it is literally true, and the tendency of a proem to slip into flattery is evident. The proem concludes with a pathetical reminder of the wrath to come, which anticipates the question to be raised in chapter 5. As a matter of crucial interest to the Thessalonians, it serves here to increase their attention to the letter as a whole.

Verses 2:1–8 are a refutation of charges against Paul, anticipating objections to his authority and thus important for his ethos in the letter. The passage is especially interesting in that it contains Paul's own characterization of his rhetoric, which he describes as courageous, without guile, intended to please God and not men, without flattery, gentle, and affectionate. These qualities seem exhibited in 1 Thessalonians, though subsequent situations were sometimes to strain them.

Verses 2:9–3:13 recast the materials of a narration in striking ethical and pathetical terms. Events are experienced rather than simply recounted. The general arrangement, as expected in a narration, is chronological, moving from Paul's first ministry in Thessalonica (2:9) to his departure for Athens (2:17) to his present circumstances (3:6). The Thessalonians themselves are cited as witnesses of what he says (2:10, 3:3), in the latter case amplified with some pathos. Early in the narration (2:11) Paul compares himself to a father, the Thessalonians to children. By the end he can claim that what in the minds of the Thessalonians was a question of their survival without him has become the question of his survival without them: "For now we live, if you stand fast in the Lord" (3:8). This remarkable reversal is secured by moving from the sufferings of the Thessalonians, equated in 2:14 with those of Jesus and the prophets, to the vivid and repeated expression of his own suffering. In 2:19 he asks "For what is our hope or joy or crown of boasting before our Lord at his coming? Is it not you?" Note how identification is assumed by the rhetorical question and how the basically simple sentence is amplified by the metaphors "crown" and "boasting," the pathetical words "hope" and "joy," and the reference to Jesus, which introduces the topic of the wrath to come. The narration, after all its emotion, ends calmly in a prayer (3:11–13).

The headings (4:1–5:22) open with a proposition in general terms (4:1), supported by the authority of Jesus (2). This is then divided into an injunction to chastity (3–8) and to love of one's neighbor (9–11). The questions bothering the Thessalonians about whether the dead are to be saved (4:13–18) and about the time of the end of the age (5:1–11) are then dealt with, followed by a chiastic return to other injunctions (5:12–22). The epilogue (5:23–24), like the conclusion of the narration, is a calm prayer. Verses 5:25–28 are the closure.

Second Thessalonians resembles 1 Thessalonians, but is much shorter and omits the narration. Second Corinthians has already been discussed in Chapter 4 and some remarks on 1 Corinthians appended to it. Further analysis of that important letter may be left to the interested student, and we may turn here to the Epistle to the Galatians, probably written around A.D. 55.

As one of the most vigorous and eloquent of Paul's epistles, Galatians is of great rhetorical interest, and it is not surprising that it has been the first of the books of the New Testament to be singled out for detailed rhetorical analysis; we now have a recent commentary by Hans Dieter Betz from which much can be learned about the epistle and about rhetoric. As it happens, something can also be learned about the pitfalls of rhetorical criticism when not practiced in accordance with the method outlined in Chapter 1, for Betz's commentary is misleading in important respects and the result is somewhat to distort interpretation of the epistle.

Betz regards Galatians as an apologetic letter and thus an example of judicial rhetoric. "Paul's defense" is repeatedly mentioned in his commentary. He was apparently led to this view, at least in part, by the existence of a narrative section in Galatians 2, a feeling that narration is characteristic of judicial rhetoric, and a resulting effort to see in the letter the traditional parts of a judicial oration as described by Quintilian and to see the letter in a traditional genre. He may also have been influenced by his own extensive knowledge of the dispute between parties in the early Church and a desire to bring out that dissension more sharply than may be immediately apparent to many readers of the Bible. Paul certainly *could* have written a defense of the charges made against him in Galatia or elsewhere; but one of the most important things to notice about Galatians is that he did not choose to do so. Instead, he preached the gospel of Christ. What the Galatians thought of Paul mattered only in that it contributed to or detracted from his authority and thus influenced their belief and actions; what they believed and how they were going to act as a result of those beliefs mattered a great deal.

All species of rhetoric make use of narrative, but they use it for different purposes and in different ways. The function of judicial narrative is to set forth the facts at issue from the point of view of the speaker. Quintilian (4.2.66–68) clearly recognizes this. But the narrative of the first and second chapters of Galatians is not an account of facts at issue. It is supporting evidence for Paul's claim in 1:11 that the gospel he preached was not from man, but from God, a topic which had been enunciated in the first verse of the salutation.

Galatians is probably best viewed as deliberative rhetoric, a point to which we will return. Quintilian discusses the use of narrative in deliberative oratory in 3.8.10–11. He thinks that a narration of the facts is not necessary when an orator has been consulted by someone other than a public body, since the facts are then usually known, but that a narration of external matters may frequently be introduced. What is meant by external matters is explained in 4.2.11–12. They are matters which have a bearing on the case and contribute to an understanding of the speaker, but are not directly at issue. This well describes the narrative in Galatians, the function of which is to establish Paul's ethos and thus to support his claim of the truth of his gospel.

The narrative of the early chapters of Galatians is not evidence that the epistle as a whole is judicial, and is consistent with a view of it as deliberative. The exhortation of 5:1–6:10 is strong evidence that the epistle is in fact deliberative in intent. This exhortation is a problem for Betz's theory, since exhortation, as he recognizes, is not regarded as a part of judicial rhetoric by any of the ancient authorities. Betz is puzzled (p. 254) by their silence and notes that exhortation, or *paraene-*

sis, is a regular feature of philosophical letters. It is, but philosophical letters like those of Seneca are not judicial: they either inculcate belief without calling for action, in which case they are epideictic, or they exhort the recipient to a particular course of action, in which case they are deliberative. Exhortation is one of the two forms of deliberative rhetoric, the other being dissuasion (see Quintilian 3.4.9). Paul exhorts the Galatians to quite specific actions, in particular to a rejection of the practice of circumcision.

Betz overemphasizes the presence of narrative and underestimates the presence of exhortation and in so doing neglects the principle of linearity, which was stressed in our outline of rhetorical criticism in Chapter 1. Galatians, like other works intended to be heard, unfolds in a linear manner. What Paul is leading to in chapters 1–4 is the exhortation of chapters 5–6. That is the point of the letter. It might be argued that the choice of deliberative form is a rhetorical stance on Paul's part, that he is trying to disguise defense as deliberation. Betz's view is close to this, for he consistently identifies rhetoric with deceit. To do so, however, is to charge Paul with hypocrisy in his remarks about his own rhetoric in 1 Thessalonians and in 1 and 2 Corinthians, as well as in his practice here, and that seems unnecessary. Paul's rhetorical stance in Galatians, including his choice of species, is explicable on the grounds that he emphasized what he thought was important.

The basic argument of deliberative oratory is that an action is in the self-interest of the audience, or as Quintilian prefers to put it, that it is right (8.3.1–3). That is the pervasive argument of Galatians. The Christian community should not observe the Jewish law and should not practice circumcision, which is now not only unnecessary, but wrong. Conversely, Christians should love one another and practice the Christian life. The letter looks to the immediate future, not to judgment of the past, and the question to be decided by the Galatians was not whether Paul had been right in what he had said or done, but what they themselves were going to believe and to do. Since Betz wrongly identifies the question at issue, he is led wrongly to identify the stasis as qualitative (p. 129). Insofar as stasis theory can be applied to deliberative rhetoric, the stasis is one of fact: What gospel is true? What should the Galatians do?

Would the rhetorical method outlined in Chapter 1 have aided and corrected Betz's interpretation of the text? Perhaps. Although it would have begun with a rather similar discussion of the rhetorical situation of the letter and Paul's exigence in writing it, it would have identified problems Paul faced and also have helped to explain what might seem to be judicial elements in terms of Paul's final objective. He has to establish his ethos, to which the narrative contributes, and he has to anticipate or refute logical objections to his view of the law, which he does in chapters 3–4. The method would have called for a more careful consideration of the species and perhaps led not only to reference to Quintilian's extended discussion of judicial rhetoric, but to his one chapter on deliberative rhetoric (3.8), which has a number of points relevant for understanding Galatians. It would have required an awareness of linear composition and the direction of movement of thought of the work, and in its final step would have included an assessment of the whole. It seems unlikely that anyone reading through Galatians at one sitting would conclude that it is an apology rather than an attempt to persuade the Galatians, swayed by other advisers, what they should do. In all critical methods there is certainly some room for difference of opinion, but there are critical principles which need to be observed to reach valid results, and in this case the significance of the epistle is at issue. As Paul's defense, Galatians would be chiefly of historical interest for its picture of the early Church filled with acrimonious dissension and of his personal insecurities and apprehensions; as Paul's exhortation it continues to speak to Christians who are tempted to substitute the forms of religious observance for its essence.

Galatians begins with a salutation (1:1–5) which is amplified by two topics important for the letter: "an apostle not from men nor through men, but through Jesus Christ and God the

Father" (1:1), which lays the basis for Paul's ethos; and "the Lord Jesus Christ, who gave himself for our sins to deliver us from the present age" (1:3), which contains within itself the kernel of the doctrine of freedom.

This is followed by a proem (1:6–10) which by its vigor immediately attracts attention and which, like the opening of Cicero's first Catilinarian oration to the Roman senate, contains a biting attack on those who would counsel otherwise. The central idea of the proem, that there is no other gospel, is a general statement of the proposition of the letter, which will be taken up and given specific meaning in the headings which follow. It is given emphasis by the figure *epidiorthosis*, or *correctio*, in verse 7 and by the reiteration in verse 9, which Betz unnecessarily claims refers to some other occasion, as well as by the invective against Paul's opponents. Betz's citation of Cicero and Quintilian on frightening the judges by curses (p. 46) is irrelevant; the curses are directed against Paul's opponents, not against the Galatians, who are the judges. Verse 10 is very interesting in that Paul here shows how rhetorically conscious he is by calling attention to the fact that his proem does not seek favor with the audience. The verse is a written aside which contributes to his ethos by its candor.

The proof, or working out of the headings, begins in 1:11–12 with Paul's restatement of the topic of the salutation: "The gospel which was preached by me is not man's gospel." This is shown to be credible by the extended narrative of 1:13–2:14. The gospel was revealed to him, and he did not confer with flesh and blood (1:16); he went to Jerusalem by revelation (2:2). The isolation of Paul from the other apostles serves to amplify their ultimate acceptance of him in 2:6–10 and thus to strengthen his ethos, while that of his opponents is undermined in 13–14 and in the following dramatic incident with Peter. Verses 2:15–21 constitute an epicheireme, or argument with the parts fully stated, which provides the conclusion to the first heading, Paul's authority, and introduces the specific issue which Paul must examine, the question of the law. The main objection to calling it a proposition, as Betz does (pp.

113–14), is that it is argumentative, and it may indeed be derived as some have believed from an earlier speech.

A second heading begins in 3:1 and may be summarized as
the claim that the gospel is true because of the experience of
the Galatians. This topic is also to be found in 4:8–11, which
thus frames an extended argument based on evidence from
Scripture and the example of a will (3:6–4:10). The Galatians'
experience of the gospel has been challenged by those who
demand observance of the law, and it is thus appropriate for
Paul to insert here a refutation of their views. Verses 3:6–18
provide the scriptural evidence for Paul's position on the law,
from which he constructs an enthymematic argument. The
true sons of Abraham, he argues, are "men of faith"; Abraham
was promised that in him "all nations" would be blessed;
therefore those who are men of faith are blessed with Abraham
who had faith. The scriptural injunction that those who do not
abide in the law are cursed is set in opposition to the injunction "He who through faith is righteous shall live." Paul is here
dealing with that form of legal stasis in which two laws are in
conflict, and his solution of the conflict is to say that Christ has
redeemed us from the curse of the law. The Scripture says,
"Cursed be everyone who hangs on a tree"; Christ has hung
upon a tree; therefore he has taken the curse upon himself.
To the pro-circumcision party this dialectical argument might
have seemed a rather arbitrary interpretation of words, as
perhaps would Paul's subsequent insistence that "offspring,"
rather than "offsprings," of Abraham must refer to Christ. It
may be a part of Paul's method to try to show that it is he who
is the strict constructionist and not his opponents.

The whole labored argument essentially rests not on the
scriptural passages cited nor on the logical acceptance of
Paul's premises by his opponents—a necessary condition in
true dialectic—but on the Galatians' acceptance of his authority in making these proclamations and their experience of
Paul's teachings. His anticipation of objections involves difficult philosophical or theological concepts which are very suc-
cinctly stated, and though they may have been clear to him,

their rhetorical function in the letter is perhaps more to seem to recognize the possibility of objections and to be prepared to answer them confidently than to provide a developed response. This is not a matter of deceit on Paul's part, but of a realistic assessment of what was likely to be the actual basis of decision on the part of his audience. What is immediately important for the Galatians is recapitulated in personal terms in 3:23–4:11, with repeated use of the personal pronoun "you."

This is followed by a personal appeal by Paul to the Galatians (4:12–20). To the ethos and logos of the previous discussion is added pathos. He makes no strong break here, for the Galatians' experience of God is dependent on their experience of Paul and his experience of God. He links these by reminding them of their kindnesses to him, sensing, as Thucydides says (2.40), that it is not our benefits to others that most secure their friendship, but their perception that we are obliged to them.

Verses 4:21–31 contain the allegorical interpretation of the story of Sarah and Hagar. Betz's discussion (pp. 239–40) seems to confuse allegory as used by a speaker and the use of allegorical interpretation in exegesis. He treats the passage as a distinct unit, but it has close ties with what has gone before and prepares for the declaration of freedom which is to follow. Throughout the proof Paul moves back and forth between the experience of the Galatians and the scriptural evidence, of which this passage is a culminating statement. He also moves from the first person singular in earlier parts of the letter to the second person plural to a first person plural identification of himself and the Galatians.

The entire section of the proof from 1:11 to 5:1 corresponds to the theological sections seen in most other epistles of Paul and provides the basis for the specific commandments which are the practical purpose of the letter. These begin with the negative injunction against circumcision in 5:2, which is complemented by the positive injunction of love in 5:14, followed by a synkrisis of the works of the flesh and the works of the spirit in 5:19–24, amplified in Paul's pleonastic style, with additional pastoral commandments. There is a complex interlocking of topics such as circumcision, the flesh, and love.

The epilogue, as Betz rightly recognizes, consists of the postscript of 6:11–18. It attacks Paul's opponents, recapitulates his most important injunction, that against circumcision (6:15), and has, as Betz suggests (pp. 323–24), some undercurrent of pathos. It is important to notice that what Paul thinks he has demonstrated to the Galatians is not that they should alter their judgment of him, but that "neither circumcision counts for anything nor uncircumcision, but a new creation" (6:15).

Aristotle defined rhetoric as the faculty of observing the available means of persuasion, and classical rhetoricians generally think an effort should be made to assemble and evaluate all possible arguments. Paul clearly does not do this. In Galatians he addresses an audience including gentiles in a hellenized province of the Roman empire, but he makes no use of the common Greek objection to circumcision as unaesthetic and unnatural, perhaps since that would be to glorify the flesh; nor does he argue on practical grounds as Peter seems to do in Acts 15, that to demand a painful rite of adult converts will inhibit the spread of Christianity. That argument might seem to denigrate the value of what was being received, and pain in an initiatory rite has some psychological appeal. There are probably other instances of Christian rejection of "available means of persuasion" which could be identified and would help to define Christian rhetoric. In any event, Christian rhetoric does not proliferate arguments in the way recommended by the rhetoricians, but focuses on a few presented as absolute in their validity. It is curious that modern American Christians who put a strict construction on other injunctions of Saint Paul do not seem passionately opposed to circumcision; this probably results from the effective rhetoric during the early twentieth century of another movement claiming absolute authority, the medical establishment, which has, however, recently begun to change its doctrine and to muster arguments against routine circumcision.

Romans is a considerably longer epistle than those we have been considering, and it resembles them in structure and in topics but is to be regarded as more epideictic in intent. Its rhetorical differences are chiefly those resulting from the different audience Paul addresses. The Thessalonians were a small congregation which he had personally founded and which he was anxious to reassure in time of trial so that its members might be exhorted to the Christian life. The Galatians were a somewhat larger community with which he had had a close personal tie, but which seemingly had turned away from the faith as he understood it and needed to be brought back; he hoped a forceful expression of this feeling would have a positive effect. But in Romans he is writing to a church which he has never visited and which has therefore never heard his gospel. The extended greetings in 16:3–15, something not met before, are thus valuable in establishing a personal tie with those he addresses: these are, as it were, his witnesses. The fuller exposition of his thought in chapters one to eleven is needed to explain the faith as he understands it. The exigence for the letter is perhaps provided by Paul's feeling that in his mission to the entire world it is important to reach the Christian community of the capital. He hopes to visit them personally, and this letter is a step in opening communications. The two main rhetorical problems he faces are his audience's lack of personal knowledge of him and the probability that there will be among them those clinging to the law and hostile to aspects of his message. He wishes to show them in advance what his gospel will be and thus to anticipate problems which might, and in fact did, arise (Acts 28:24–29). It is interesting that he does not make an effort at the outset to establish his personal ethos, perhaps by a narrative of his conversion. He asserts and illustrates, but does not justify his claim to be an apostle until the epilogue. This could be regarded as a subtle appeal to the Romans; they are assumed to take an ecumenical view suitable for the capital of the world. He does not directly tackle the possibility of faction either, but in chapter 1 inveighs against those within the Greek tradition who have always rejected God's will and in chapter 2 sets up an imaginary Jewish opponent to refute.

Like other letters we have considered, Romans has two main parts: the first, chapters 1–11, is doctrinal and contains both the positive message and the refutation of objections; the second, chapters 12–15, is the pastoral application of this doctrine. The short proem (1:8–15) seeks the goodwill of the Romans by giving thanks to God for the fame of their faith and by stressing Paul's goodwill toward them, seen in his desire to visit them. In addition to faith (verses 8, 12), the topics of spirit (9, 11), the gentiles (13), and the gospel (15) are touched on.

Then comes the proposition of the letter as a whole (1:16–17): the gospel is the power of God for salvation to everyone who has faith, to the Jew first and also to the Greek. Paul's initial declaration of his pride in the gospel is figured as a litotes, "not ashamed of the gospel." Although this is an ethical introduction to the proposition, rather than one of its terms, and reminiscent of the courageous *persona* projected by Paul in other letters, it sounds a note which is echoed in the use of the first person singular throughout the letter. The proposition is given enthymematic form by the reason adduced in verse 17, supported by quotation from Scripture.

The various terms in the proposition—power of God for salvation, everyone who has faith, Jew first, then Greek—are a partition underlying the structure of 1:18–11:36. Throughout the epistle Paul turns back and forth between an audience of Jews and one of gentiles, seeking tolerance. Generally speaking, he may be said to begin with "the power of God for salvation" and its opposite, the power of God for damnation, treated in a narration in 1:18–2:16. This is then followed (2:17–4:25) by headings centering on the situation of the Jew and then (5–6) the gentile. Chapter 7 is at first addressed to the

Jews, but then broadened to establish the nature of faith, ending with the triumphant proclamation of 8:37–39, that nothing
can separate us from the love of God in Christ Jesus our Lord.
In this section Paul repeatedly poses and answers questions.
Verses 9:1–11:36 are addressed to gentiles to provide an understanding of the situation of Jews. This is given its own introduction by Paul speaking personally as a Jew (9:1–6), its own
striking proposition (God has not failed his word to Israel,
9:6), and its own conclusion (11:36), and it is appropriately rich
in scriptural quotation.

The pastoral headings (12:1–15:13) are unusually broad, as
seen for example in the list at 12:6–8. Since they are largely
concerned with belief and attitude, not with action, they do
not, as elsewhere, convert the letter into deliberative rhetoric.
The injunctions of chapter 12 are for the most part authoritatively pronounced "by the grace given to me" and not supported by argument or Scripture, until verse 19. In chapters 13,
14, and 15, however, injunctions are more frequently cast as
enthymemes with supporting statements or are accompanied
by examples or scriptural citation.

The epilogue (15:14–33) resumes points made in the proem,
but is more personal in tone and has elements of a narration—
of events to come. It is here, rather than at the beginning of
the letter, that Paul seems to be justifying his apostolic mission. At the outset of the letter he assumes authority which is
then given a reality in the power of his thought throughout
the following chapters. By the end it is well established in both
a spiritual and intellectual sense, and he gives it an authentic,
pathetical ring by combining proclamation of his pride in the
gospel with a final appeal for the prayers of the Romans as he
faces confrontation in Jerusalem. Chapter 16:1–23 is a postscript, which as noted above is effective in establishing personal relationships with individuals he believes to be in Rome.
The final three verses of the epistle are the closure of the letter,
given some amplification by reference to the topics of the salutation: the gospel; to all nations; for the obedience of faith.

The style of Romans is relatively sophisticated, doubtless

reflecting Paul's perception of what is appropriate to a Roman audience. It contains in 5:3–5 a splendid example of climax (a figure of thought), and its use of his characteristic pleonasm, as in 1:29–31, shows a carefully controlled ability to arrange words to express emotion. Rhetorical questions maintain audience contact in strategic locations, as in 2:21–23. Paradoxical wordplay underlines the argument, as in 4:18 or 6:20, without becoming sophistical.

At least since Bultmann's study (1910), influences of the diatribe upon Romans have been noted. The diatribe is not a literary genre, in the sense of genre understood by classical grammarians and rhetoricians, but it does have some claims to be regarded as a form with distinctive traditions. What we said about generic criticism in Chapter 1 is applicable here. Knowledge of the characteristics of a diatribe may be useful in understanding the rhetorical situation as Paul perceived it and why he chose some rhetorical techniques rather than others. Although we cannot say with confidence that the Christian community of Rome was better educated than the Christian community of Corinth, it is reasonable to think that Paul may have expected a Roman audience to have a greater degree of literacy than, say, the Christians of Thessalonica. Certainly techniques of diatribe are far more conspicuous in Romans than in other epistles.

What a diatribe is, what features of Romans are reminiscent of a diatribe, and how this knowledge may be useful in understanding Romans has recently been much clarified by Stanley K. Stowers. He argues that a diatribe is not, as commonly believed, a popular philosophical sermon of the sort attributed to wandering Cynic or Stoic philosophers, but a type of discourse occasionally employed by a teacher in a philosophical school in which he addresses and rebukes his students and refutes logical objections to his doctrines which they have made or might make. The techniques of diatribe were sometimes used in published works, for example by Dio Chrysostom and Plutarch, or diatribes of a teacher were written up by a student, as Arrian did with those of Epictetus. Classical works described in antiquity as diatribes have the atmosphere of the schoolroom. The teacher can be very pointed in his criticisms of students, but his sternness must be understood in terms of his concern for and even love of his students. Romans is not a diatribe, but it makes use of the technique of diatribe in its attacks on the boastful and pretentious. These should not be regarded as specific, unnamed people; they are types. The effect is thus quite different from the kind of polemic in which Paul engages with opponents in Corinth or Galatia. He is offering the Roman church an example of the kind of preaching or teaching he will practice when among them. The individuals to whom he sends affectionate greetings in chapter 16 are persons with whom he has had the kind of teacher–student relationship associated with use of the diatribe.

Although rhetorical criticism can cast light on the unity of a letter, as with 2 Corinthians, it does not seem to be adequate to establish or disprove authenticity of a letter as a whole, as with Ephesians. If Ephesians is not by Paul, it is by someone of considerable rhetorical skill who was determined to produce a letter which Paul could have written. The Epistle to the Hebrews, however, is clearly by a different hand and makes no claim to Pauline authority. Although it does include at the end a chapter of pastoral injunctions, it lacks proem, the personality of the author is almost totally hidden throughout, and that intricate interplay of topics, characteristic of Paul, is not conspicuous. A contrast of the great eleventh chapter, the most extended example of anaphora in the New Testament, to the thirteenth chapter of 1 Corinthians is instructive of the differences of rhetoric. Paul's encomium of love is personal and nervous, emotional at the beginning, but quieter at the end as the emotional energy is dissipated; the encomium of faith in Hebrews 11 is historical and objective, building great dignified blocks of thought toward an emotional expression as the end approaches.

Chapter Eight. Conclusion

Twentieth-century thought as seen in some of its most original philosophers, writers, and artists, as well as at the frontiers of theoretical science, points towards a conclusion that mankind cannot know reality, at least not directly or not under contemporary conditions. At most, it is argued, we can know structures, words, and formulae perhaps representative of aspects of reality. Even if an individual were to perceive reality experientially or intuitively, there is some pessimism whether this understanding can be communicated through the media available to us to any general segment of the population. I do not share this view in its more extreme forms; an eventual new synthesis of knowledge may well be achieved containing a subtler perception of being arising from humanistic and scientific research and from individual genius, but it is certainly true that reality is more elusive in our time than it seemed in the eighteenth or nineteenth century. The new synthesis, if it can be effected, may well take another century or more.

In biblical studies historical criticism, form criticism, structuralism, and other methods have, at least for many readers, seemed to move us further away from a sense of certainty about what actually happened in the formation of Christianity. Not only the historical Jesus, but the personalities of Matthew and John and the veracity of events, or of the interpretation of events, set forth in Acts have faded under analysis, while our understanding of Paul has become increasingly complex. Even devout Christians now sometimes accept the use of the term "myth" to describe Christianity. Mythical need not mean "false," and it means "fictitious" only in the root sense of that word: "creative." Religious truth, and even some scientific truth, is greater than the power of the human mind to comprehend. God may reveal himself in the Bible, but since his nature is by definition infinite it is impossible for it to be fully revealed through a finite medium to a finite mind. This creates the necessity for myth, which seeks to picture the infinite in terms human beings can grasp. In that process, myth uses human narrative as an analogy for divine narrative, and it describes varying aspects of the infinite through metaphor. Jesus himself does this constantly in the parables. Kenneth Burke's imaginative book *The Rhetoric of Religion* may provide some readers with insight into the analogies between words and the Word which are characteristic of religious discourse.

If the Bible is in a sense mythical, it is even more necessary to regard it as rhetorical, again not in the sense of "false" or "deceitful," but in the sense of "purposeful," as a form of communication, perhaps between God and man, certainly between biblical writers and ourselves. All religious systems are rhetorical: they are attempts to communicate perceived religious truth, just as political discourse is an attempt to communicate perceived political doctrine and is necessarily rhetorical. Philosophical systems are equally rhetorical: some, like Platonism or the philosophy of Leibniz, create a grand myth as a vision of truth; others, like logical positivism, are more modest in their goals but still seek to convey an impression of reality. Even science needs rhetoric and resorts to myth-making, for example in picturing general hypotheses such as those relating to the origin and nature of the universe or the evolution of life.

Rhetoric is a more comprehensive phenomenon than myth-making, for myth is only one of several possible forms of communication. Others include proclamation, based on external authority, and conceptual argument, as well as the persuasive uses of ritual, music, and the arts, which have a rhetoric of their own to move the mind or the emotions. For some readers of the Bible rhetorical criticism may have an appeal lacking to other modern critical approaches, in that it comes closer to explaining what they want explained in the text: not its sources, but its power. Rhetoric cannot describe the historical

Jesus or identify Matthew or John; they are probably irretrievably lost to scholarship. But it does study a verbal reality, our text of the Bible, rather than the oral sources standing behind that text, the hypothetical stages of its composition, or the impersonal workings of social forces, and at its best it can reveal the power of those texts as unitary messages. The Bible speaks through ethos, logos, and pathos, and to understand these is the concern of rhetorical analysis.

A striking result of the present study is recognition of the extent to which forms of logical argument are used in the New Testament. Though sacred language stands behind this, inherent in many of the utterances of Jesus, and though a tradition of radical, nonlogical discourse survived in the Church and still exists in modern existentialism and fundamentalism, even in the first century a process was underway of recasting expressions in enthymematic form, thus making sacred language into premises which are supported, at least in a formal sense, by human reasoning. The workings of the human mind significantly changed in the centuries preceding the Christian era because of the conceptualization of thought in Greece and the spread of Greek culture throughout the East. The New Testament lies not only at the cusp of Judaism and Hellenism, but at a cusp in Jewish and Hellenic culture where thought in myths confronts thought in logical forms. Some modern philosophers, or antiphilosophers, regard logical analysis and exegesis as a negative factor in civilization which has vitiated human efforts to comprehend reality. But "those things which can be learned from men should be learned without pride," Augustine argues in the Prologue to *On Christian Doctrine*. "The condition of man would be lowered if God had not wished to have men supply his word to men." It is rhetoric that supplies word to men, as Augustine well knew, and it is conceptualized rhetoric that describes that process.

Sacred language affects to be outside of time, but the very process of casting it into words casts it into history. Words create and reflect their culture, and to read them outside that culture is to invite a basic level of misunderstanding. That is why Augustine demanded that exegesis begin with a knowledge of language and history. Much the same is true of rhetorical conventions; there is need for some knowledge of classical rhetoric in reading the New Testament. To cite cases discussed in this book, it is not clear that readers of the New Testament have grasped that the rhetorical function of the Beatitudes, *as they stand in the text of Matthew*, is that of a proem, or that narrative passages in the Bible are often ethical proofs, or that Paul regularly enunciates a proposition which is worked out in a series of topics. We have seen several cases in which translators of the Bible have failed to realize how individual words or sentences work rhetorically, and places where modern paragraphing is rhetorically faulty. Doubtless more instances will come to light with continued analysis.

Some may feel that the emphasis of rhetorical criticism on hearing the texts as an early Christian audience heard them is a limiting factor which may obscure the universal meaning of the text for modern readers. But this objection is more applicable to historical or form criticism, both of which tend to ignore the existence of a specific audience; an awareness of classical rhetoric, if properly used, may become a tool to penetrate those features of the text which are culture-specific and to allow those which are universally valid to stand forth with greater clarity. The Latin Vulgate and the King James Version are also to some degree culture-specific. To read them without an awareness of the language of their times compounds the difficulty of understanding their message not only to contemporaries, but to us. Classical rhetoric was one of the constraints under which New Testament writers worked, analogous to the historical constraints recently identified by A. E. Harvey. Rhetorical analysis thus might be compared to the process of translating the Scriptures for modern readers, a task necessitated every generation or two by the continual change in our ways of hearing words. As a result of such efforts of scholarship the religious truths of the Bible can be made more easily available to the general reader, and its powerful impact on Christians can be better understood.

Bibliography

PRIMARY SOURCES

Although varying in quality, the most convenient editions of classical rhetoricians, when they exist, are those in the Loeb Classical Library published in Cambridge by Harvard University Press and in London by William Heinemann. Editors' names and publication dates are indicated below. Each volume includes the original text and an English translation, index, and varying amounts of introductory material and notes.

Aristotle
> *The "Art" of Rhetoric*, by J. H. Freese, 1926.
> *Topica*, by E. S. Forster, 1960. (In the volume with Aristotle, *Posterior Analytics*.)

Cicero
> *Brutus*, by G. L Hendrickson, 1939.
> *Orator*, by H. M. Hubbell, 1939. (In the volume with *Brutus*.)
> *De Inventione, De Optimo Oratorum*, and *Topica*, by H. M. Hubbell, 1949.
> *De Oratore* and *De Partitione Oratoria*, by E. W. Sutton and H. Rackham, 2 vols., 1942.

Demetrius
> *On Style*, by W. Rhys Roberts, 1932. (In the volume with Aristotle, *Poetics*.)

Longinus
> *On the Sublime*, by W. Hamilton Fyfe, 1932. (In the volume with Aristotle, *Poetics*.)

Quintilian
> *Institutio Oratoria*, by H. E. Butler, 4 vols., 1920–22.

Rhetorica ad Herennium
> By Harry Caplan, 1954. (This edition, one of the most valuable for the student of rhetoric, is sometimes catalogued under "Cicero, pseudonymous works," sometimes under "Auctor ad Herennium.")

Other useful translations include:

Augustine
> *On Christian Doctrine*, by D. W. Robertson, Jr. The Library of the
> Liberal Arts. Indianapolis: Bobbs-Merrill, 1958.

Bede
> "Concerning Figures and Tropes," translated by G. H.
> Tannenhaus. In *Readings in Medieval Rhetoric*, edited by Joseph
> M. Miller, Michael H. Proser, and Thomas W. Benson, pp. 96–
> 122. Bloomington and London: Indiana University Press, 1973.

Boethius
> *De Topicis Differentiis*, translated, with notes and essays on the text,
> by Eleanore Stump. Ithaca and London: Cornell University
> Press, 1978.

Hermogenes
> "*On Stases*: A Translation with an Introduction and Notes," by
> Raymond E. Nadeau. *Speech Monographs* 31 (1964): 361–424.
> *On Ideas of Style* [a partial translation]. In *Ancient Literary
> Criticism: The Principal Texts in New Translations*, edited by
> D. A. Russell and M. Winterbottom, pp. 561–79. Oxford:
> Clarendon Press, 1972.

Menander Rhetor
> Edited with translation and commentary by D. A. Russell and
> N. G. Wilson. Oxford: Clarendon Press, 1981.

The student of the rhetoric of the Bible may also be interested in a
curious fifteenth-century Hebrew rhetoric, *The Book of the Honey-
comb's Flow*, by Judah Messer Leon, edited and translated by Isaac Ra-
binowitz (Ithaca and London: Cornell University Press, 1982).
Messer Leon sought to teach classical rhetoric out of the Old Testament and used the system as a method of exegesis of biblical texts.

SECONDARY SOURCES

The following list includes works cited in the text above and some
additional studies which are likely to be of interest to the practitioner
of rhetorical criticism.

Betz, Hans Dieter. *Galatians: A Commentary on Paul's Letter to the
Churches in Galatia*. Philadelphia: Fortress Press, 1979.

_____. "The Literary Composition and Function of Paul's Letter to the Galatians." *New Testament Studies* 21 (1975): 353–79.

_____. "The Sermon on the Mount: Its Literary Genre and Function." *Journal of Religion* 59 (1979): 285–97.

Bitzer, Lloyd F. "The Rhetorical Situation." *Philosophy and Rhetoric* 1 (1968): 1–14.

Bullinger, Ernest W. *Figures of Speech Used in the Bible Explained and Illustrated*. London, 1898. Reprint Grand Rapids: Baker Book House, 1968.

Bultmann, Rudolf. *Der Stil der paulinischen Predigt und die kynischstoische Diatribe*. Göttingen: Vandenhoeck & Ruprecht, 1910.

Burke, Kenneth. *The Rhetoric of Religion: Studies in Logography*. Berkeley and Los Angeles: University of California Press, 1970.

Caird, G. B. *The Language and Imagery of the Bible*. Philadelphia: Westminster Press, 1980.

Church, F. Forrester. "Rhetorical Structure and Design in Paul's Letter to Philemon." *Harvard Theological Review* 61 (1978): 17–33.

Corbett, Edward P. J. *Classical Rhetoric for the Modern Student*. New York: Oxford University Press, 1965.

Dodd, C. H. *The Apostolic Preaching and Its Developments*. Chicago, 1937. Reprint, 2nd ed., New York: Harper & Row, 1965.

Donfried, K. P. "False Propositions in the Study of Romans." *Catholic Biblical Quarterly* 36 (1974): 332–55.

Frye, Northrop. *The Great Code: The Bible and Literature*. New York and London: Harcourt Brace Jovanovich, 1981.

Frye, Roland Mushat. *Perspective on Man: Literature and the Christian Tradition*. Philadelphia: Westminster Press, 1961.

Funk, Robert W. *Language, Hermeneutic, and Word of God: The Problem of Language in the New Testament and Contemporary Theology*. New York: Harper and Row, 1966.

_____. *Parable and Presence: Form of the New Testament Tradition*. Philadelphia: Fortress Press, 1982.

Gitay, Yehoshua. *Prophecy and Persuasion: A Study of Isaiah 40–48*. Forum Theologiae Linguisticae, 14. Bonn: Linguistica Biblica, 1981.

Grassi, Ernesto. *Rhetoric as Philosophy: The Humanist Tradition*. University Park and London: Pennsylvania State University Press, 1980.

Harvey, A. E. *Jesus and the Constraints of History*. London: Duckworth, 1982.

Jewett, Robert. "Romans as an Ambassadorial Letter." *Interpretation* 36 (1982): 5–20.

Johnson, Marshall D. *The Purpose of the Biblical Genealogies, with Special Reference to the Setting of the Genealogies of Jesus.* Cambridge: Cambridge University Press, 1969.

Judge, E. A. "Paul's Boasting in Relation to Contemporary Professional Practice." *Australian Biblical Review* 16 (1968): 37–50.

Kennedy, George A. *The Art of Persuasion in Greece.* Princeton: Princeton University Press, 1963.

———. *The Art of Rhetoric in the Roman World.* Princeton: Princeton University Press, 1972.

———. *Classical Rhetoric and Its Christian and Secular Tradition from Ancient to Modern Times.* Chapel Hill: University of North Carolina Press, 1980.

———. *Greek Rhetoric under Christian Emperors.* Princeton: Princeton University Press, 1983.

———. *Quintilian.* New York: Twayne, 1969.

Koenig, Eduard. *Stilistik, Rhetorik, Poetik in Bezug auf die biblische Literatur.* Leipzig: T. Weicher, 1900.

Lausberg, Heinrich. *Handbuch der literarischen Rhetorik: Eine Grundlegung der Literaturwissenschaft.* 2 vols. Munich: Max Hueber, 1960.

Lund, Nils Wilhelm. *Chiasmus in the New Testament: A Study in Formgeschichte.* Chapel Hill: University of North Carolina Press, 1942.

Lundbom, Jack R. *Jeremiah: A Study in Ancient Hebrew Rhetoric.* Society of Biblical Literature, SBL Dissertation Series, 18. Missoula, Montana: Scholars Press, 1975.

Mainberger, G. K. "Der Leib der Rhetorik." *Linguistica Biblica* 51 (1982): 71–86.

Martin, Josef. *Antike Rhetorik: Technik und Methode.* Handbuch der Altertumswissenschaft, 2.3. Munich: C. H. Beck, 1974.

Muilenberg, James. "Form Criticism and Beyond." *Journal of Biblical Literature* 88 (1969): 1–18.

Norden, Eduard. *Agnostos Theos: Untersuchungen zur Formgeschichte religiöser Rede.* Leipzig, 1913. Reprint Stuttgart: Teubner, 1956.

———. *Die antike Kunstprosa vom VI. Jahrhunderts vor Christus in die Zeit der Renaissance.* Leipzig: Teubner, 1909.

Perelman, Chaim, and Olbrechts-Tyteca, L. *The New Rhetoric: A Treatise on Argumentation.* Translated by John Wilkinson and

Purcell Weaver. Notre Dame, Indiana: Notre Dame University Press, 1969.

Prideaux, John. *Sacred Eloquence: The Art of Rhetoric as it is Laid Down in Scripture*. London: George Sawbridge, 1659.

Rhetorical Criticism: Essays in Honor of James Muilenberg. Edited by Jared J. Jackson and Martin Kessler. Pittsburgh: Pickwick Press, 1974.

Stowers, Stanley Kent. *The Diatribe and Paul's Letter to the Romans*. Society of Biblical Literature, SBL Dissertation Series, 57. Chico, California: Scholars Press, 1981.

Weiss, Johannes. "Beiträge zur paulinischen Rhetorik." In *Theologische Studien*, Festschrift for Bernhard Weiss. Edited by C. R. Gregory et al. Göttingen: Vandenhoeck & Ruprecht, 1897.

Wilder, Amos. *The Language of the Gospel: Early Christian Rhetoric*. New York: Harper & Row, 1964.

Wuellner, Wilhelm. "Paul's Rhetoric of Argumentation in Romans." *Catholic Biblical Quarterly* 38 (1976): 330–51.

Index